Joseph

Joseph, the viceroy of Egypt, is recognized by his brothers.

Money at its Best: Millionaires of the Bible

Abraham and Sarah
Daniel
David
Esther
Jacob
Job

Joseph
Moses
Noah
Samson
Solomon
Wealth in Biblical Times

MONEY
at its
BEST

Joseph

Benjamin T. Hoak

Mason Crest Publishers
Philadelphia

Produced by OTTN Publishing.
Cover design © 2008 TLC Graphics, www.TLCGraphics.com.

Mason Crest Publishers
370 Reed Road, Suite 302
Broomall PA 19008
www.masoncrest.com

Copyright © 2009 by Mason Crest Publishers. All rights reserved.
Printed and bound in the United States of America.

First printing

1 3 5 7 9 8 6 4 2

Library of Congress Cataloging-in-Publication Data

Hoak, Benjamin T.
  Joseph / Benjamin T. Hoak.
      p. cm. — (Millionaires of the Bible)
  Includes bibliographical references (p.   ) and index.
  ISBN 978-1-4222-0472-6 (alk. paper)
  ISBN 978-1-4222-0847-2 (pbk. : alk. paper)
  1. Joseph (Son of Jacob) I. Title.
  BS580.J6H63 2008
  222'.11092—dc22
                                                    2008011688

Publisher's Note: The Web sites listed in this book were active at the time of publication. The publisher is not responsible for Web sites that have changed their address or discontinued operation since the date of publication. The publisher reviews and updates the Web sites each time the book is reprinted.

Table of Contents

Joseph and His Wealth   6
Introduction: Wealth and Faith   7
1. Dreamer, Prisoner, and Ruler   11
2. Growing Up   17
3. Betrayal and Slavery   28
4. The House of Potiphar   38
5. The Prisoner Who Interprets Dreams   49
6. From Slave to Ruler   59
7. The Brothers Return   70
8. Joseph Revealed   80
9. Israelites in Egypt   90
10. Last Days   103

Notes   114
Glossary   117
Further Reading   119
Internet Resources   121
Index   122
Illustration Credits   127
About the Author   128

Joseph and His Wealth

- Joseph was the favorite son of Jacob, a very wealthy man. In biblical times, wealth was measured by huge flocks of sheep or goats, extensive landholdings, large families, and unlimited staffs of servants. Jacob's flocks were so large that he could afford to give a generous gift to his estranged brother Esau. Joseph's childhood, therefore, would not have been lacking in the material comforts available at the time.

- When Joseph was 30 years old, the pharaoh of Egypt—the wealthiest country of the ancient world—made Joseph his second-in-command, giving him fine clothes and generous gifts.

- According to a Jewish folktale, Joseph received gifts not only from Pharaoh, but also from the people of Egypt: "The king gave him fields and vineyards as a present, and also three thousand talents of silver, and a thousand talents of gold, and onyx stones and bdellium, and many other costly things. The king commanded, moreover, that every Egyptian give Joseph a gift, else he would be put to death. A platform was erected in the open street, and there all deposited their presents, and among the things were many of gold and silver, as well as precious stones." In addition, Joseph lived in an opulent palace that took three years to build and was decorated with gold, silver, and precious stones.

- During seven years of famine, Joseph had access to practically all the wealth of the region: "Joseph collected all the money that was to be found in Egypt and Canaan in payment for the grain they were buying, and he brought it to Pharaoh's palace" (Genesis 47:14).

- Despite the vast sums of money he handled, Joseph never cheated Pharaoh or took anything he had not earned: "Joseph displayed such excessive good faith and honesty in all his dealings, that though the time and the circumstances of the time gave him innumerable opportunities of making money, so that he might, in a short period, have become the richest man of that age or kingdom, he . . . stored up all the silver and gold which he collected, not appropriating a single drachm of it to his own use," wrote the Jewish commentator Philo of Alexandria.

- A Jewish legend holds that before his death, Joseph divided his vast fortune. He gave some of the money to his brothers and their families. The rest, consisting of gold, silver, and precious stones, was buried in four places. Part of the fortune was discovered, but, according to the legend, the other half "will never be found, because God has reserved the riches they hold for the pious, to be enjoyed by them in the latter days, the days of the Messiah."

Introduction: Wealth and Faith

Many people believe strongly that great personal wealth is incompatible with deep religious belief—that like oil and water, the two cannot be mixed. Christians, in particular, often feel this way, recollecting Jesus Christ's own teachings on wealth. "Do not store up for yourselves treasures on earth, where moth and rust destroy, and where thieves break in and steal," Jesus cautions during the Sermon on the Mount (Matthew 6:19). In Luke 18:25, he declares, "It is easier for a camel to go through the eye of a needle than for a rich man to enter the kingdom of God"—a sentiment repeated elsewhere in the Gospels.

Yet in Judeo-Christian culture there is a long-standing tradition of material wealth as the manifestation of God's blessing. This tradition is amply reflected in the books of the Hebrew Bible (or as Christians know them, the Old Testament). Genesis 13:2 says that the patriarch Abram (Abraham) "had become very wealthy in livestock and in silver and gold"; the Bible makes it clear that this prosperity is a gift from God. Other figures whose lives are chronicled in

Genesis—including Isaac, Jacob, Joseph, Noah, and Job—are described as both wealthy and righteous. The book of Deuteronomy expresses God's promise of prosperity for those who obey his commandments:

> If you fully obey the Lord your God and carefully follow all his commands I give you today, the Lord your God will set you high above all the nations on earth.... The Lord will grant you abundant prosperity—in the fruit of your womb, the young of your livestock and the crops of your ground—in the land he swore to your forefathers to give you. (Deuteronomy 28:1, 11)

A key requirement for this prosperity, however, is that God's blessings must be used to help others. Deuteronomy 15:10–11 says, "Give generously . . . and do so without a grudging heart; then because of this the Lord your God will bless you in all your work and in everything you put your hand to." The book of Proverbs—written during the time of Solomon, one of history's wealthiest rulers—similarly presents wealth as a desirable blessing that can be obtained through hard work, wisdom, and following God's laws. Proverbs 14:31 promises, "The faithless will be fully repaid for their ways, and the good man rewarded for his."

Numerous stories and folktales show the generosity of the patriarchs. According to Jewish legend, Job owned an inn at a crossroads, where he allowed travelers to eat and drink at no cost. When they offered to pay, he instead told them about God, explaining that he was simply a steward of the wealth that God had given to him and urging them to worship God, obey God's commands, and receive their own blessings. A story about Abraham says that when he moved his flocks from one field to another, he would muzzle the animals so that they would not graze on a neighbor's property.

After the death of Solomon, however, the kingdom of Israel

was divided and the people fell away from the commandments God had mandated. The later writings of the prophets, who are attempting to correct misbehavior, specifically address unethical acts committed to gain wealth. "You trample on the poor," complained the prophet Amos. "You oppress the righteous and take bribes and you deprive the poor of justice in the courts" (Amos 5:11, 12). The prophet Isaiah insists, "Learn to do right! Seek justice, encourage the oppressed. . . . If you are willing and obedient, you will eat the best from the land; but if you resist and rebel, you will be devoured by the sword" (Isaiah 1:17, 19–20).

Viewed in this light, the teachings of Jesus take on new meaning. Jesus does not condemn wealth; he condemns those who would allow the pursuit of wealth to come ahead of the proper relationship with God: "No one can serve two masters. . . . You cannot serve both God and money" (Matthew 6:24).

Today, nearly everyone living in the Western world could be considered materially wealthier than the people of the Bible, who had no running water or electricity, lived in tents, walked when traveling long distances, and wore clothing handmade from animal skins. But we also live in an age when tabloid newspapers and trashy television programs avidly follow the misadventures of spoiled and selfish millionaire athletes and entertainers. In the mainstream news outlets, it is common to read or hear reports of corporate greed and malfeasance, or of corrupt politicians enriching themselves at the expense of their constituents. Often, the responsibility of the wealthy to those members of the community who are not as successful seems to have been forgotten.

The purpose of the series MONEY AT ITS BEST: MILLIONAIRES OF THE BIBLE is to examine the lives of key figures from biblical history, showing how these people used their wealth or their powerful and privileged positions in order to make a difference in the lives of others.

A scene from a pharaoh's tomb, believed to have been painted around the time that Joseph lived in Egypt, shows an Egyptian dignitary. The staff and cord, as well as his larger size, signify this person's importance.

1

Dreamer, Prisoner, and Ruler

The account of Joseph, son of the Old Testament patriarch Jacob, provides one of the most remarkable life stories in a Bible filled with remarkable events. Joseph does not survive a flood, cause the sun to stand still in the sky, raise a child from the dead, or get swallowed by a big fish. In fact, his story is surprisingly miracle free. Nevertheless, millions have found the story compelling because of the enduring themes of integrity, forgiveness, and faith that echo through the dramatic highs and lows of Joseph's life. More than once, Joseph endures a grievous injustice, but he never descends into bitterness or self-pity, and he never loses hope. His fortitude and faith preserve the life of the infant nation of Israel, and his legacy of righteousness resounds through three major world religions: Judaism, Christianity, and Islam.

Joseph

Joseph is usually remembered as the boy with the coat of many colors, and for good reason. The 11th of the 12 sons of Jacob, Joseph is his father's favorite from the beginning, and it shows in gifts like the multicolored coat. This favoritism leads to much resentment on the part of his brothers. When Joseph is 17 years old, they almost kill him before deciding to sell him to slave traders bound for Egypt.

Once in Egypt, Joseph serves in the house of the captain of Pharaoh's guard. Thrown headlong into a new culture, he earns the privilege of managing the captain's entire estate; nothing is held back from him. Eventually, the captain's wife tries to seduce him. He resists firmly, so she accuses him of attempted rape. Flung into prison for a crime he did not commit, Joseph faces the prospect of spending the rest of his life wasting away. But his talent again becomes plain to see, and the jailer puts the entire prison in Joseph's charge. While in prison, Joseph interprets dreams for two dismissed servants of Pharaoh, the king of Egypt. Later, Pharaoh himself summons Joseph to interpret his own difficult dreams.

After Joseph does so—the dreams foretell seven years of plenty followed by seven years of famine—Pharaoh immediately installs Joseph as his chief minister, in charge of managing all of Egypt's land. Thus a lowly foreign slave has worked his way up to command an empire.

The famine Joseph predicted does indeed arrive, and because of it Joseph's brothers eventually come to Egypt to buy grain. Joseph recognizes them and, after testing them, reveals who he is and gives them his forgiveness. Jacob and his family then move to Egypt, where Joseph provides for them until his death.

His story is one of passion, pride, fear, and faith. It is an account that excites the mind and emotions. Anger, intrigue, attempted murder, slave trading, false accusations, years in prison, and a startling rise to prominence all play a role. There is forgiveness, redemption, and hope—concepts that all humankind can understand.

FULFILLING THE COVENANT

But the life of Joseph is more than just an inspiring story about a random family. Joseph's great-grandfather Abraham is the father of the Jewish nation and the man with whom, Jews and Christians believe, God made a covenant:

> And God said to [Abraham], "Behold, my covenant is with you, and you shall be the father of a multitude of nations. . . . I will make you exceedingly fruitful, and I will make you into nations, and kings shall come from you. And I will establish my covenant between me and you and your offspring after you throughout their generations for an everlasting covenant, to be God to you and to your offspring after you. And I will give to you and to your offspring after you the land of your sojournings, all the land of Canaan, for an everlasting possession, and I will be their God." (Crossway Bibles: English Standard Version, 2001; Genesis 17:3–8)

To keep the covenant, God grants Abraham a son named Isaac, born late in Abraham's life. Isaac has twin sons, Jacob and Esau, and Jacob has 12 sons—Joseph and his brothers, the fathers of the 12 tribes of Israel. From those humble beginnings, the Jewish nation would multiply to include millions upon millions of people.

Joseph becomes a crucial instrument in the survival of the Jewish people—and thus in the fulfillment of the covenant God had made with Abraham. If not for Joseph, the famine that surged across the land might have snuffed

14 Joseph

Colorful scenes from Joseph's life appear in the pages of this French illuminated manuscript from the 14th century. Jewish, Christian, and Muslim traditions all consider Joseph an important figure.

out Abraham's descendants—the nation of Israel—when they constituted just a few dozen souls. In the midst of that famine, a desperate Jacob sends his sons to the one place he knows there is food: Egypt, where according to Psalm 105:16–17, God had sent Joseph to prepare the way ("When he [God] summoned a famine on the land and broke all supply of bread, he had sent a man ahead of them, Joseph, who was sold as a slave"). If not for Joseph, Pharaoh would not have understood the significance of his dreams and ordered preparations for the famine. If Joseph had not stored grain ahead of time, Jacob would have had nowhere to turn for food. Without food, the nation of Israel would have been lost.

LIFE LESSONS

The theme of God's providential hand figures prominently in the narrative of Joseph. The Bible and Jewish legends speak repeatedly of God directing the events of Joseph's life—even the seemingly inexplicable ones—for a purpose: to preserve the life of a nation. Joseph's unshakeable trust in God's guiding hand is also evident throughout the various accounts of his life. His statement to his brothers at the end of Genesis—"You meant it for evil, but God meant it for good" (Genesis 50:20)—has become a classic testimony of faith.

A second distinct quality of Joseph—one that Jewish rabbis often point out—is his ability to maintain his identity as a Jewish believer throughout a long life in a completely foreign culture. Joseph spends 93 of his 110 years in Egypt, but he takes his identity and his belief system from the first 17 years of his life. He excels in his new surroundings and even blends in, but he never loses sight of who he is. This theme is repeated over and over again throughout the Old Testament—Jews succeeding in a culture outside their own while remaining true to their own beliefs and culture.

The story of Joseph also offers a lesson in the power of forgiveness to change lives. Joseph's brothers have committed great evil against him, but he does not return evil for evil or hold their guilt over them. Rather, he forgives them, loves them, and brings them to live with him. His merciful treatment of those who have done him violent wrong provides a model for generations to follow.

The account of Joseph's life is the longest single narrative in the book of Genesis (chapters 37 and 39 through 50). In the Qur'an an entire sura, or chapter, is given over to Joseph. Pages upon pages of Jewish tales are devoted to him as well. Joseph is one of the few main characters in

Scripture about whom almost nothing negative is written. His character is beyond reproach, so much so that Jewish sages call him *Yosef ha-Tzaddik*, or "Joseph the Righteous."

Joseph's tremendous power and influence in Egypt enable him to help his people survive the famine. His position as Pharaoh's trusted minister certainly gives him access to great personal wealth as well. Jewish legends do include stories about Joseph's riches, including his palatial house and his fine clothes. Yet there is no hint of greed on Joseph's part, no suggestion that he ever acquires wealth through dishonest means. On the contrary, Joseph's story is one of honest, capable stewardship of the vast resources placed under his control.

Most of the story of Joseph concerns his life from age 17 to 39. There is also a glimpse of him at 56 and a brief portrait at 110, as his life comes to an end. Throughout, this dreamer, prisoner, and ruler demonstrates remarkable faith, and his example has had a lasting impact on untold numbers of believers.

Jewish legends are tales that have been told over the centuries but that do not come directly from the Tanakh, or Jewish Bible. They are often derived from the Talmud (an authoritative collection of Jewish laws and legal decisions, along with commentary) and the Midrash (stories that expand on Bible incidents, to illustrate legal or moral principles). Rabbis often used the Midrash to fill in gaps in the Torah (the first five books of the Tanakh). These collective stories are also called *Haggadah*, the Hebrew word for legends of the Bible.

Growing Up

Joseph's lifetime, nearly 2,000 years before the birth of Jesus Christ, bridges the era of the patriarchs in the land of Canaan and the era of the Hebrew people in Egypt. To fully understand his story, it is necessary to examine the life of his father, Jacob. Much of the conflict that shapes Joseph's life can be traced to the actions of Jacob.

Jacob's History

Jacob, the last of the great Jewish patriarchs, is the son of Isaac and the grandson of Abraham. His birthplace, Canaan, is the land promised by God to Abraham.

Although he learns to trust and follow the God of his fathers, Jacob displays a cunning, manipulative streak. He swindles his brother Esau out of his birthright and tricks his father into giving him the blessing that belonged to Esau. Later,

18   *Joseph*

Jacob sets out to find a wife in the distant land of Paddan-aram (in upper Mesopotamia, to the northeast of Canaan), where his mother's relatives live. On the way, God appears to him in a vision and renews the covenant with Abraham:

> I am the Lord, the God of Abraham your father and the God of Isaac. The land on which you lie I will give to you and to your offspring. Your offspring shall be like the dust of the earth, and you shall spread abroad to the west and to the east and to the north and to the south, and in you and your offspring shall all the families of the earth be blessed. Behold, I am with you and will keep you wherever you go, and will bring you back to this land. (Genesis 28:13–15)

In response, Jacob vows to follow God and keep the covenant. When he reaches his destination, he meets a man named Laban and falls in love with his daughter Rachel, who the Bible says is beautiful in form and appearance. Jacob agrees to work seven years for Rachel's hand in marriage, and his love makes the seven years pass quickly. The day after the wedding, however, he wakes to find that Laban has deceived him—he is married not to Rachel, but to her older sister Leah, who is not as attractive. (It was the custom of the time to cover a bride's face until morning.) Still very much in love with Rachel, Jacob marries her a week later after agreeing to work an additional seven years for the privilege.

In the end, he works 14 years for two wives. It was not unusual in that time for men to have more than one wife, although the situation could cause problems. It does in Jacob's case—he loves Rachel more than Leah, which leads to jealousy and conflict.

Leah has an advantage over her sister, though. She produces children, while Rachel is unable to do so. Being barren was a severe stigma for women of that culture, and Rachel struggles deeply with her inability to bear children. As was common, she provides her maid Bilhah to bear children in her place, and Bilhah produces two sons. Leah does the same, and her maid Zilpah bears two sons as well. Leah herself gives birth to six sons and one daughter.

The Bible says that after many years, God remembered Rachel and opened her womb so that she gave birth to Joseph. In Hebrew, his name means "may He add," or "He has added"—the "He" referring to God. Jacob showers love and attention on Joseph, whose existence takes on even more meaning for Jacob when his beloved wife Rachel dies while giving birth to her second son,

Jacob observes Rachel at a well while watching the flocks of Laban, her wealthy father. Rachel and Jacob would eventually marry. This illustration is by the 19th-century French artist Gustave Doré.

Benjamin. Jacob pours all his grief and love for her into Joseph, even to the neglect of his other children.

The final named tally of Jacob's children includes 12 sons: Reuben, Simeon, Levi, Judah, Dan, Naphtali, Gad, Asher, Issachar, Zebulun, Joseph, and Benjamin. He also has one daughter, Dinah.

Twenty years after his arrival in Mesopotamia seeking a wife, Jacob decides the time is right to take his wives and children back to Canaan. Although the Bible does not say exactly how wealthy he has become, Jacob is clearly a man of means. Genesis 30:43 says, "Thus the man increased [prospered] greatly and had large flocks, female servants and male servants, and camels and donkeys. . . . Jacob heard that the sons of Laban were saying, . . . 'he has gained all this wealth.'"

When he returns to Canaan, he reconciles with his brother Esau by first offering a gift of 550 choice goats,

A herd of sheep walks through a desert area near Galilee, in the modern-day state of Israel. In the Middle Eastern culture of antiquity, a person's wealth was typically determined by the size of his herds of livestock.

Wrestling with an Angel

While on his journey from Mesopotamia back to the land of Canaan, Jacob spends an entire night wrestling with an angel of the Lord, understood to be God incarnate. Jacob wrestles fiercely and will not let go without a blessing; at the end of the night, the angel declares that his name will no longer be Jacob ("one who takes by the heel or supplants"), but Israel ("he who strives with God"). The name change is a tribute to Jacob, moving him from a past of deception to a future of honor before God.

Later, just before Rachel dies while giving birth to Benjamin, God appears to Jacob and reiterates the name change to "Israel"—which will also be the name of the nation that descends from him. "A nation and a company of nations shall come from you, and kings shall come from your own body," God says. "The land that I gave to Abraham and Isaac I will give to you, and I will give the land to your offspring after you" (Genesis 35:11).

ewes, rams, camels, cows, bulls, and donkeys. If he can afford to give such a large present, the flocks and herds he has in reserve must be vast. Later Esau moves away from Jacob, "for their possessions were too great for them to dwell together. The land of their sojournings could not support them because of their livestock" (Genesis 36:7).

Exchangeable money had not yet fully developed, so animals were just as valuable to their owners as their equivalent value in silver or gold would have been. As *The Anchor Bible Dictionary* puts it, "Abraham and the other patriarchs counted their wealth in numbers of sheep, goats, and cattle. . . . Throughout the period of the patriarchs and into the time of the kings of Israel and Judah, the primary means of commerce and trade was barter. Money could be metallic and weighed . . . or it could be in kind."

Jacob must have had a large number of servants as well. Genesis 14:14 records that Abraham, who was also wealthy, had at least 318 trained men (servants or bodyguards) as part of his household.

Two Bible incidents in particular show that although he is wealthy, Jacob tends to be passive as a father; these events help explain how he could let his family spiral so out of control that his sons will sell their own brother into slavery. First, there is the account, in Genesis 34, of the rape of Jacob's daughter, Dinah, by the prince of Shechem, a city in the land of Canaan where Jacob's family is lodging. When their father does not respond to this crime, Dinah's brothers take matters into their own hands. Simeon and Levi kill all the males in the city, after which their brothers plunder Shechem. When he hears of this, an angry Jacob upbraids Simeon and Levi. "Should he treat our sister like a prostitute?" they ask him in reply (Genesis 34:31).

The second incident that illustrates Jacob's passivity as a father comes when his firstborn son, Reuben, sleeps with Bilhah, Jacob's concubine. Jacob fails to discipline Reuben for this evil deed. The Bible simply says, "And Israel [Jacob] heard of it" (Genesis 35:22).

FAVORED SON

It is against this backdrop that Joseph enters fully onto the scene in chapter 37 of Genesis. He is 17 years old, living in the land of Canaan and working as a shepherd. Among his brothers, resentment of Joseph is festering:

> Jacob lived in the land of his father's sojournings, in the land of Canaan. These are the generations of Jacob. Joseph, being seventeen years old, was pasturing the flock with his brothers. He was a boy with the sons of Bilhah and Zilpah, his father's

wives. And Joseph brought a bad report of them to their father. Now Israel loved Joseph more than any other of his sons, because he was the son of his old age. And he made him a robe of many colors. But when his brothers saw that their father loved him more than all his brothers, they hated him and could not speak peacefully to him. (Genesis 37:1–4)

Reuben is Jacob's firstborn son, and yet the passage skips straight to Joseph when it begins describing Jacob's generations. That is surely a mark of Joseph's favored status, as well as an indication that he will ultimately rise to greater prominence than any of his brothers.

Several factors have played into Jacob's favoritism of Joseph. The primary reason seems to be Jacob's greater love of Rachel than of Leah. Yet Benjamin is also a son of Rachel; perhaps her death during Benjamin's birth has caused Jacob to be emotionally distant from his youngest son. Josephus, a Jewish commentator and historian of the first century C.E., says that Jacob also loved Joseph both because of the "beauty of his body and the virtues of his mind, for he excelled the rest in prudence." A traditional Jewish legend suggests that Joseph "resembled his father most closely in appearance," and that the entire course of his life echoed that of Jacob's. Legend also says that Joseph became so learned by the age of 17 that he could teach even his older brothers. One scholar says that perhaps Joseph's talent went a long way toward explaining Jacob's affections: "It was not unnatural for Jacob to have a special affection for Joseph . . . because that interesting mixture of grace and talent which afterwards shone out in him so remarkably, and which was such a contrast to the coarseness of his brothers, had won his heart, and had knit the souls of father and son into a wonderful unity."

If Joseph enjoys his father's love, he also endures his brothers' hatred. Jacob is not subtle about his favoritism toward Joseph, and his brothers seethe with anger, indignation, and jealousy. Josephus says that the "affection of his [Joseph's] father excited the envy and the hatred of his brethren." They surely envy his coat of many colors, an elaborate garment of great distinction that was most likely long sleeved and full length—not something a man would wear while working hard in the fields and herding flocks each day. Archaeologists have found an Egyptian wall painting dating to about 1900 B.C.E. that depicts just such a coat. This kind of garment conferred favor and elevated status upon the one who wore it; a father usually gave it to the son he intended to lead the household one day. By giving the coat to Joseph and raising the younger brother above the older brothers, Jacob has broken with the patrilineal tradition of passing on titles, privileges, and inheritances to the firstborn son. Joseph's brothers know this, and they hate the coat and all that it represents.

The apocryphal Testament of Simeon bears witness to the hatred Simeon—a leader in the plot against Joseph—carries for his brother. "For in the time of my youth I was jealous in many things of Joseph, because my father loved him beyond all," Simeon says. "And I set my mind against him to destroy him because the prince of deceit sent forth the spirit of jealousy and blinded my mind, so that I regarded him not as a brother, nor did I spare even Jacob my father" (Simeon 1:7–8).

According to the Qur'an, when the brothers realize how important Joseph is in their father's eyes, they begin to make plans not just to ignore him, but to kill him: "Surely Joseph and his brother [Benjamin] are dearer to our father than ourselves, though we are many. Truly, our father is much mistaken. Let us slay Joseph, or cast him away in some far-off land, so that we may have no rivals in our father's love, and after that be honourable men" (The Koran, translated with notes by N. J. Dawood, 1993; Qur'an 12:8–9). Their opportunity would come soon enough.

SPOILED BRAT, OR PRINCIPLED SON?

The character and motivations of the young Joseph are open to interpretation. Some people see him as a "spoiled brat, constantly capitalizing on his most-favored-son status" and intentionally antagonizing his brothers (for example, by flaunting his coat). Others believe that he tries his best to be honorable and to please God and his father, though he is undeniably naïve in his dealings with his rough-and-ready brothers.

It does seem that Joseph brings on at least some of his brothers' resentment by carrying reports of their bad behavior back to his father. The Bible does not mention specifically what Joseph says about them. However, in the apocryphal Testament of Gad, Joseph is said to have reported that Gad and his brothers—the sons of Zilpah and Bilhah—were killing and eating the best animals of the flock (including a lamb that had been attacked by a bear and would not have survived anyway). "And regarding this matter I was wroth with Joseph until the day that he was sold," Gad says. "And the spirit of hatred was in me, and I wished not either to hear of Joseph with the ears, or see him with the eyes, because he rebuked us to our faces saying that we were eating of the flock without Judah. For whatsoever things he told our father, he believed him" (Gad 1:8–10).

According to another interpretation, Joseph's brothers hate him mainly because his upright character makes them feel guilty for their own less-than-perfect actions. In this view, Joseph cannot help but tell his father of his

"Then Joseph had another dream, and he told it to his brothers. 'Listen,' he said, 'I had another dream, and this time the sun and moon and eleven stars were bowing down to me.'" (Genesis 37:9).

brothers' misdeeds—both because of his own disappointment in their actions and because of his close relationship with Jacob. Yet the shame the brothers feel only increases their hatred of Joseph.

Only in Dreams

Even if Joseph's intentions are always good, he occasionally displays a bit of youthful foolishness and arrogance. Nowhere is this clearer than in the way Joseph deals with his dreams. Dreams (and more specifically, the interpretation of pairs of dreams) will become an integral part of Joseph's life. But when his first nighttime visions arrive, he is not experienced enough to think that perhaps he needs to be cautious in what he reveals.

In Joseph's first dream, he and his brothers are binding sheaves of grain in the field; Joseph's sheaf stands upright while the other sheaves gather around it and bow down. Immediately after having the dream, Joseph tells his brothers of it. Their reaction is predictable: "'Are you indeed to reign over us? Or are you indeed to rule over us?' So they *hated him even more*" (Genesis 37:8, emphasis added).

Joseph does not seem to take the hint from his brothers' indignant reaction to his dream. He has another dream, which he quickly shares with his brothers—and, this time, with his father as well. In this second dream, the sun, moon, and 11 stars are bowing down to Joseph. Even Jacob is taken aback at this revelation. "What is this dream that you have dreamed?" Jacob asks in Genesis 37:10. "Shall I and your mother and your brothers indeed come to bow ourselves to the ground before you?"

Despite his astonishment, Jacob keeps the dream in mind—hinting, perhaps, that he believes the dream might come true (as indeed it does, many years later). Joseph's brothers, on the other hand, are furious. They are jealous of him, craving the power and prestige that has apparently been promised to Joseph. They do not realize that true greatness might come through humility, by submitting to God's plan. Two decades will pass before they learn this lesson.

Betrayal and Slavery

Sometime after Joseph reveals his dreams to his brothers, Jacob sends them to pasture his flocks near Shechem (the same city where Dinah had been raped). Joseph does not go with them—possibly another instance of favorable treatment by his father—but Jacob sends him later to check on the men and bring back word of their situation. He thinks it will be a short trip for Joseph; as events turn out, he will not see his son again for more than 20 years.

The Brothers' Revenge

Joseph travels about 50 miles north from the Valley of Hebron (where Jacob has settled) to Shechem. But upon his arrival there, he wanders the fields, unable to find his brothers. Then a man tells him that they have moved to a town called Dothan, which is located 15 miles to the north.

Joseph's brothers see him approaching

from a distance (a task made easier by his brightly colored coat) and quickly devise a plan to kill the "dreamer" and throw him into a pit. This is not just idle chatter—the brothers' malice is unmistakable, and they even discuss how they will explain Joseph's disappearance: "We will say that a fierce animal has devoured him, and we will see what will become of his dreams" (Genesis 37:20). The historian Josephus speculates that the brothers actually resolved to kill Joseph before they left home with the flock; as part of their plan, they deliberately moved from Shechem, in order to entice Jacob to send Joseph out alone in search of them.

Ultimately Reuben—perhaps because he feels some responsibility as the firstborn son—prevents the murder of Joseph by suggesting that the brothers just throw him into the pit. (Reuben intends to come back later to rescue his brother and restore him to his father.) When Joseph arrives, his brothers strip off his hated coat and fling him into a pit that had been used as a cistern before running dry. Such pits exist even today; they are built

This illustration from a Flemish book of the 15th century shows Joseph being thrown into a well by his brothers.

with a narrow mouth and sides that bulge out like a wide jar—all but impossible to escape from. Legend has it that the pit was swarming with snakes and scorpions and that the brothers stripped Joseph bare and flung stones at him.

Joseph is in a desperate spot. While his brothers sit down to a meal, he faces his worst fears, as one scholar describes:

> In such a place he was left to die—under the ground, sinking in the mire, his flesh creeping at the touch of unseen slimy creatures, in darkness, alone . . . in a species of confinement which tames the most reckless and maddens the best balanced spirits, which shakes the nerve of the calmest. . . . A few wild cries, that ring painfully round his prison, show him he need expect no help from without; a few wild and desperate beatings round the shelving walls of rock show him there is no possibility of escape. He covers his face, or casts himself on the floor of his dungeon to escape within himself; but only to find this also in vain, and to rise and renew efforts he knows to be fruitless. Here, then, is what is come of his fine dreams. With shame he now remembers the beaming confidence with which he had related them; with bitterness he thinks of the bright life above him, from which these few feet cut him so absolutely off, and of the quick termination that has been put to all his hopes.

As it happens, the brothers are camping on a trade route between Syria and Egypt. According to archaeologists who have investigated the site, Dothan was most likely a major slave market in the second millennium B.C.E. It is not surprising, then, that a caravan of traders bound for Egypt comes along. The traders' camels are laden with gum, balm, and myrrh. Perhaps stirred by a twinge of conscience, Judah proposes selling their brother to the traders in lieu of murdering him and having his blood upon their hands. Judah's suggestion foreshadows a plea he will make two decades later, when he begs Joseph to take him, rather than their brother Benjamin, prisoner.

The brothers agree to Judah's plan and sell Joseph to the traders for 20 shekels of silver, the average price of a slave at the time. There is some confusion as to whether the traders are Ishmaelites or Midianites—they are called both in the Bible's account. One interpretation says that the descendants of Ishmael (Abraham's son by the servant girl Hagar) and of Midian (Abraham's son by his second wife, Keturah) were so intermingled that they were called by either name; it could also be that the traders were a mixed band including groups of both people.

THE AFTERMATH

Reuben is away when his brothers sell Joseph. The Bible does not say where; Jewish legend says he is hiding in the mountains so that he can rescue Joseph at an opportune moment. When he returns and finds Joseph gone, Reuben tears his clothes in grief for his brother; he also knows that his father will hold him, as the firstborn, responsible for

---

In ancient Egypt, people typically became slaves in one of two ways: either they were sold on the slave market or they were captured during a war. The life of Egyptian slaves is depicted in detail on tomb paintings of wealthy Egyptians. One document from an Egyptian household around 1740 B.C.E. lists 79 domestic servants, over half of whom have Semitic names such as Jacob, Issachar, and Asher.

This 16th-century painting depicts Joseph (in blue clothing) being handed over to the slave traders. "[Judah,] seeing some Arabians . . . carrying spices and Syrian wares out of the land of Gilead to the Egyptians, . . .advised his brothers to draw Joseph out of the pit, and sell him to the Arabians; for if he should die among strangers a great way off, they should be freed from this barbarous action," wrote Flavius Josephus in his history *Jewish Antiquities*.

Joseph's disappearance. The brothers recognize that they will have to explain Joseph's absence to their father, so they slaughter a goat and dip Joseph's robe in the blood, creating the impression that he has been devoured by a wild animal.

They send the robe back to Jacob, asking him to identify whether or not it is Joseph's—as if they would not recognize the garment that has caused so much ill will. Even with Joseph out of the way, they are still calculating and cruel, tricking their father into thinking his beloved son has been brutally killed. Jacob is grief-stricken at the loss of Joseph: "Then Jacob tore his garments and put sackcloth on his loins and mourned his son many days. All his sons and all his daughters rose up to comfort him, but he refused to be comforted and said, 'No, I shall go down to Sheol [the place of the dead] to my son, mourning.' Thus his father wept for him" (Genesis 37:34–35). His sons try to comfort him, but they fail to offer the one thing that could bring true relief to Jacob's heart—the truth. Ironically, Jacob is suffering because his sons have perpetrated the same sort of deceit on him that he perpetrated on his own father many years before, when he tricked Isaac into bestowing on him the blessing that was meant for Esau.

The Bible does not say what Joseph's brothers do with the 20 shekels of silver they have obtained in exchange for Joseph. They certainly do not need the money, as their father is a wealthy man. Several ancient texts, however, mention that the brothers spend the money on shoes. Zebulun says in his apocryphal testament, "Simeon and Gad and six other of our brethren took the price of Joseph, and bought sandals for themselves, and their wives, and their children, saying: We will not eat of it, for it is the price of our brother's blood, but we will assuredly tread it under foot, because he said that he would be king over us, and so let us see what will become of his dreams" (Zebulun 1:18–19). An Aramaic translation of the Hebrew Bible adds, "And they sold Joseph to Arabs for twenty pieces of silver and they bought shoes with them" (Targum Pseudo-Jonathan, Genesis 37:28).

This legend probably comes from another book of the Old Testament. Amos 2:6 says, "For three transgressions of Israel, and for four, I will not revoke the punishment, because they sell the righteous for silver, and the needy for a pair of sandals." Amos is not referring to Joseph (he is rebuking Israel for sin). But over time, the passage became applied to the story of Joseph.

This detail from a 13th-century Byzantine-style mosaic, which ornaments a church in Florence, Italy, shows Joseph's brothers presenting the bloodstained coat to their parents. The Jewish philosopher Philo of Alexandria (ca. 20 B.C.E.–ca. 50 C.E.) described Jacob's grief in great detail: "Nothing has ever happened more intolerable than this misfortune which has now befallen me; which has consumed and destroyed all the vigour of my soul; for what can be a greater or more pitiable calamity? [Joseph's death will] afflict me with a never to be forgotten and never ending sorrow."

Wealth in Ancient Times

Before the Hebrew people first used coins (sometime around the fifth century B.C.E.), precious metals such as gold and silver were weighed for their value rather than counted out as money. Some units of weight later became the name of a coin.

The word *shekel* is actually the Hebrew word for weight. In the ancient Jewish system, a common shekel weighed about 0.4 ounces (or about 11.3 grams). Joseph's brothers sold him for 20 silver shekels, the average price of a slave at the time. To put it into perspective, one silver shekel was equal to four days' wages for a common laborer.

Although the approximate value of biblical currency can be expressed in modern money, exact conversions are not possible because the buying power of money has fluctuated so much since ancient times.

JOURNEY TO EGYPT

During the caravan journey to Egypt, Joseph would have had plenty of time to contemplate his bleak future—the route extended nearly 400 miles over difficult, barren terrain. Scholars have traced two ancient routes of slave traders from western Asia to Egypt. One sticks close to the coastline of the Mediterranean Sea. The other stays east of the Jordan River from Damascus, skirts the Dead Sea, and then cuts westward across the Sinai Peninsula to Egypt.

Joseph is known as a man of integrity and righteousness upon whom the blessing of God rests. One Jewish legend that deals with Joseph's journey to Egypt carries this to an amusing extreme, however. Joseph's "body emitted a pleasant smell," the legend says, "so agreeable and pervasive that the road along which he travelled was redolent thereof, and on his arrival in Egypt the perfume from his body spread over the whole land, and the royal princesses, following the sweet scent to trace its source, reached the place in which Joseph was." Apparently, Joseph was so blessed that he made the entire land of Egypt smell pleasant!

The last verse of Genesis 37 describes Joseph's fate after the Ishmaelite caravan arrives in Egypt: he is sold to Potiphar, the captain of the guard and an officer of

Dating Joseph's Time in Egypt

Establishing dates for Joseph's time in Egypt is difficult, if not impossible. Some scholars place Joseph in Egypt during the reign of the Hyksos (ca. 1730 to 1570 B.C.E.). A Semitic tribe from Canaan known as the "shepherd kings," the Hyksos were racially and culturally related to the Hebrews and would presumably have been friendly with them. Some evidence—including burial sites, pottery, and building styles—links the Hyksos period to the time the Israelites spent in Egypt. A Semitic king in power would help explain Joseph's ascendance and Pharaoh's immediate acceptance of Joseph's family (who were shepherds) when they came to Egypt.

Other scholars date Joseph's time in Egypt to the 12th dynasty (ca. 1991-1786 B.C.E.), which was part of the Middle Kingdom period of Egyptian history. They argue that the cultural clues from the biblical account point to Egyptian, not Semitic, rulers. For example, the names in the Joseph narrative are Egyptian (also, it is difficult to imagine why a Hyksos pharaoh would give Joseph an Egyptian name, as occurs in Genesis 41:45). Furthermore, Joseph shaves before his audience with Pharaoh (Genesis 41:14), but a Hyksos king would not have been offended by a beard. Finally, when Joseph's brothers first come to Egypt, they openly discuss their dilemma in front of him (not realizing who he is); if they thought he was a Hyksos ruler, they would have known he did not need an interpreter to understand their confidential conversation.

Pharaoh, the king of Egypt. Joseph would have been taken to the city where Pharaoh lived. Scholars have traditionally identified this as On, which the Greeks called Heliopolis, the "City of the Sun." Some people, however, believe the city was Tanis or Zoan, near the land of Goshen in northeast Egypt.

Even as a new slave, Joseph's outstanding character attracts the attention of powerful and influential people. As one scholar notes, "That there was something superior about him [Joseph]—a gentleness and refinement above the calling of shepherds that fitted him for the higher grades of slave-service—may be inferred from his being purchased as a house-servant by Potiphar, captain of the guard to Pharaoh."

According to Jewish legend, Potiphar is willing to pay as much as 400 pieces of silver for Joseph. While the price seems high to him, it is not too much for a slave who pleases him as much as Joseph. In fact, the legend goes, Potiphar demands that the traders produce proof that Joseph is actually a slave, for he appears to be of noble blood and Potiphar wants to be sure that he has not been kidnapped. The Qur'an records that Potiphar's opinion of Joseph is so high that he tells his wife to be kind to him, for "he may prove useful to us, or we may adopt him as our son" (Qur'an 12:21).

Joseph's life is beginning to look up. Indeed, things will go extremely well for a while. But when Joseph refuses to compromise his beliefs in the face of extreme temptation, everything will come crashing down, leaving him worse off than when he was sold into slavery.

THE HOUSE OF POTIPHAR

Joseph is a slave in a foreign land. He does not know the language, customs, or culture of Egypt. He sees no familiar faces. He is not tending sheep and wearing a fancy coat anymore. Seemingly nothing in his 17 years could prepare him for this new life.

Success in Potiphar's House

Remarkably, however, Joseph is prepared. As will happen many times throughout his life, Joseph excels when plunged into a brand-new setting. He has a unique ability—though at this point it is still not fully developed—to assess a situation and determine the best course of action. More important, though, Joseph has the Lord. Five times in the first five verses of Genesis 39, the Bible refers to the Lord's presence or blessing on Joseph and all his activities. "The Lord was with Joseph. . . . His master saw that the Lord was with him and that the Lord caused all that he did to succeed in his hands ... the Lord blessed the Egyptian's house for Joseph's sake; the blessing of the Lord was on all that he had" (Genesis 39:2–5). Joseph is not left to flounder helplessly in a new land. The God that he believes in, the God of his fathers, has equipped him to excel in whatever he does. The Qur'an says that God, who has power over all things, established Joseph in Egypt, "and when he reached maturity We [God] bestowed on him wisdom and knowledge" (Qur'an 12:22).

Joseph adjusts quickly to his new home. When Potiphar realizes that the Lord's blessing is upon whatever Joseph does, he places Joseph in charge of his affairs. In addition to being favored by God, Joseph succeeds by using his talents—including wisdom, discernment, and good business sense. He works hard to master the language, learn the customs, and manage Potiphar's estate.

That estate would likely have been quite extensive, given Potiphar's high position in Pharaoh's administration. Egyptian estates of the time were surrounded by a large wall with a main entrance gate. Inside the compound were a small temple and formal gardens, with a large central two-story main home, complete with a roof garden. Behind the main house could have been a slaughterhouse, stables, a bakery and brewery, grain silos, a

This sphinx—carved from white stone and boasting the face of an ancient ruler—was found at Memphis, the capital of Egypt during the period of Hyksos rule.

kitchen, and slave quarters. Joseph would most likely have started out in a humble section of the estate. Only by dint of his talent and hard work would he have moved up the ranks until he oversaw the day-to-day management of the entire operation. In that role, Joseph would have learned Egyptian methods of administration, land management, and accounting—all skills that would serve him well when he came to rule Egypt in future years.

Joseph proves himself to be so capable and trustworthy with Potiphar's affairs that the only thing Potiphar concerns himself with is the food he eats. Everything else he places under Joseph's care.

POTIPHAR'S WIFE

The Bible describes Joseph at this point as "handsome in form and appearance" (Genesis 39:6). The phrase "hand-

Joseph (at right) speaks with the Egyptian official Potiphar (center).

some in form" is used only three times in the entire Old Testament; the other two usages describe King David and his son Absalom. Joseph's physical appearance is the subject of numerous tales and legends. The Qur'an and Jewish tales both record instances in which Potiphar's wife, to show other women of the city Joseph's beauty, invites them over for a meal. She serves oranges and gives each guest a knife with which to cut her orange. Upon seeing Joseph, the women are so entranced by his visage that, according to the legend, "they all cut their hands with the knives, and the oranges in their hands were covered with blood, but they, not knowing what they were doing, continued to look upon the beauty of Joseph without turning their eyes away from him."

"God preserve us!" the Qur'an records them saying. "This is no mortal, but a gracious angel" (Qur'an 12:31).

Potiphar's wife is in the house with Joseph day after day, and she grows increasingly attracted to him. Egyptian women were among the most liberated of the ancient world, and Potiphar's wife finally approaches Joseph directly and says, "Lie with me" (Genesis 39:7). Although many men in his position might have jumped at the chance to commit adultery with a beautiful woman, he refuses, saying:

> Behold, because of me my master has no concern about anything in the house, and he has put everything that he has in my charge. He is not greater in this house than I am, nor has he kept back anything from me except yourself, because you are his wife. How then can I do this great wickedness and sin against God? (Genesis 39:8–9)

It cannot have been easy to resist her temptation. Joseph is in his twenties, strong, handsome, and single.

The Hebrew word used here for "refused" is *va-ye-ma-ain*; when the Torah is read aloud in a Jewish synagogue, the reader uses a musical note for the word, which occurs only three times in the entire Torah. The word is drawn out in the chant (it lasts about five seconds), indicating that it was a struggle for Joseph to say no to Potiphar's wife.

But he does indeed say no. His refusal to sleep with Potiphar's wife stems from two reasons: his loyalty to his master and his sense of right and wrong before God. He will not repay Potiphar's trust by taking the one thing that Potiphar has held back from him. Nor will Joseph commit a sin against his God.

Even though Joseph has firmly rebuffed her initial advance, Potiphar's wife insistently pursues him day after day. In the Jewish tale of Joseph and Zuleika (the traditional name for Potiphar's wife), several pages are filled with descriptions of her attempts to seduce him with magic spells, threats, flattery, gifts, and arguments. At one point, the tale recounts an occasion when Zuleika tries to seduce Joseph in her bedroom, where an idol sits. Knowing that what she wants to do is wrong, she covers the eyes of the idol. Joseph's response is pure righteousness: "Though thou coverest up the eyes of the idol, remember, the eyes of the Lord run to and fro through the whole earth."

Joseph stands firm as the temptress continues her relentless campaign. The Bible says he "would not listen to her, to lie beside or to be with her" (Genesis 39:10).

The Testament of Joseph describes several ploys by Potiphar's wife to entice Joseph to sleep with her, including her scheme to follow his God: "And she said unto me [Joseph]: If thou willest that I should leave my idols, lie with me, and I will persuade my husband to depart from his idols, and we will walk in the law by thy Lord. And I said unto her: The Lord willeth not that those who reverence Him should be in uncleanness, nor doth He take pleasure in them that commit adultery, but in those that approach Him with a pure heart and undefiled lips" (Testament of Joseph 1:40–41).

The matter finally reaches a breaking point one day when the house is deserted except for Potiphar's wife, and Joseph walks in to attend to his work. The Bible does not say why no one else is around; Jewish legend says Potiphar's wife has feigned sickness to stay home from a festival that all the other members of the household are attending. Knowing that she and Joseph are alone, she grabs him by his coat, saying, "Lie with me." Joseph realizes that words will not dissuade her now, so he takes the

Beauty in Ancient Egypt

Women in ancient Egypt used makeup to beautify themselves. Potiphar's wife—as a member of the upper class—presumably has access to the finest cosmetics available at the time, including eye shadow, eyeliner, rouge, and lip coloring. Of her, the apocryphal Testament of Joseph says, "She was very beautiful, splendidly adorned in order to beguile me" (Testament of Joseph 1:80).

Several pieces of ancient Egyptian jewelry, from the collection of the British Museum.

only available option—leaving his garment in her hands, he flees the house. The original Hebrew language of the Bible literally means that he left his garment and went to the street. The book of Jubilees says his determination to escape was so strong that he "broke the door and ran away from her to the outside" (Jubilees 39:8–9).

Realizing that she will have some explaining to do when her husband comes home, Potiphar's wife quickly concocts a plausible lie and tries it out on the men of her household: "See, he [Potiphar] has brought among us a Hebrew to laugh at us. He came in here to lie with me, and I cried out with a loud voice. And as soon as he heard that I lifted up my voice and cried out, he left his garment beside me and fled and got out of the house" (Genesis 39:14–15). Her story, in addition to being a complete fabrication, includes a dash of racism (she makes sure to identify Joseph as a Hebrew) and subtly places blame on her husband, who is responsible for bringing Joseph into the household. Ancient legends also say that she gathered friends to accuse Joseph of the same actions against them.

The Bible says that when Potiphar hears of the incident, his anger is kindled, and he throws Joseph into the royal prison. Despite this, it might be inferred that Potiphar does not entirely believe his wife. He is one of the highest-ranking officials in all of Egypt, a man of great wealth and power. As the captain of the guard (literally, the captain of the executioners), he can have a prisoner executed with no questions asked—and it seems likely that he would do precisely that if he truly believed that a slave had attacked his wife. Thus it seems reasonable to conclude that, having seen Joseph's character over several years—and perhaps knowing his wife's character as well—Potiphar realizes that there is more to the story than his wife is telling. Nevertheless, he cannot let such a public accusation go unpunished, so he imprisons Joseph.

In the Qur'an, suspicion quickly falls on Potiphar's wife. After Joseph denies her advances, saying, "Wrongdoers shall never prosper" (Qur'an 12:23), she accuses him of rape and he denies the charge. Her servants conclude, quite logically, that if the shirt Joseph left in the house is torn from the front, Potiphar's wife is telling the truth. If, however, it is torn from the back (which would have happened as he turned to flee), then she is lying. Qur'an 12:28 records the results of the

"When his master heard the story his wife told him, saying, 'This is how your slave treated me,' he burned with anger. Joseph's master took him and put him in prison, the place where the king's prisoners were confined" (Genesis 39:19–20). Detail from a 14th-century Florentine mosaic showing Joseph being thrown into prison.

46 *Joseph*

This illustration from a 15th-century Arabic manuscript shows Potiphar's wife tearing the back of Joseph's coat as he flees from her.

investigation: "And when her husband saw that Joseph's shirt was rent from behind, he said to her: 'This is but one of your tricks. Your cunning is great indeed! Joseph, say no more about this. Woman, ask pardon for your sin.'" Later in the Qur'anic story, Potiphar's wife actually confesses to Pharaoh that she falsely accused Joseph.

Although he has acted righteously and is completely blameless, Joseph is punished—even in the Qur'anic story, in which his innocence has been publicly demonstrated. After being wrenched away from his comfortable life as his father's favorite son and cast into slavery, he has over the course of several years assiduously proved his worth as

The Story of Two Brothers

An Egyptian tale that was written down on a papyrus dating to about 1225 B.C.E. closely resembles the story of Joseph and Potiphar's wife. Although some of the details vary, the tale is called the "Story of Two Brothers" and features a married older brother, Anpu (or Anepu or Anubis), and his younger brother, Bata (both brothers are named after Egyptian gods). One day Anpu sends his brother in from the fields on an errand. When Bata gets to the house, Anpu's wife attempts to seduce him, saying, "There is great strength in thee, for I see thy might every day."

Bata angrily refuses his brother's wife, saying, "What is this wickedness that thou hast said to me? Say it not to me again. For I will not tell it to any man, for I will not let it be uttered by the mouth of any man."

When Anpu returns home that evening, his wife is upset. When he asks her why she is distressed, she implies that Bata made dishonorable advances toward her. Furious, Anpu sets out to kill his brother with a knife. Before he does so, Bata manages to convince him of the truth, whereupon Anpu returns home and kills his wife instead.

the business manager of one of Egypt's most important officials—only to wind up being thrown into prison for a crime he did not commit. The Bible is silent on how Joseph feels about this devastating turn of events, but it is not difficult to imagine his anguish as he faces the prospect of years, perhaps even a lifetime, in prison.

THE PRISONER WHO INTERPRETS DREAMS

When Joseph is thrown into prison—which is variously described as "the house of the captain of the guard" (Genesis 40:3), "his master's house" (Genesis 40:7), and a "pit" or a "dungeon" (Genesis 40:15, 41:14), he is only in his mid-twenties. This is the second major reversal of fortune he has endured in less than a decade. Yet he remains faithful to his religious beliefs. And, as Genesis 39:21–23 makes clear, God remains with Joseph:

> But the Lord was with Joseph and showed him steadfast love and gave him favor in the sight of the keeper of the prison. And the keeper of the prison put Joseph in charge of all the prisoners who were in the prison. Whatever was done there, he was the one who did it. The keeper of the prison paid no attention to anything that was in Joseph's charge,

because the Lord was with him. And whatever he did, the Lord made it succeed.

These verses sound remarkably similar to the account of Joseph's first days in the house of Potiphar. Again God ensures that everything Joseph undertakes will succeed. Perhaps Joseph recognizes this, as there is no hint of complaining or disgruntlement on his part.

Jewish legend paints a similar picture:

> Seeing the youth's zeal and conscientiousness in executing the tasks laid upon him, and under the spell of his enchanting beauty, he [the jailer] made prison life as easy as possible for his charge. He even ordered better dishes for him than the common prison fare, and he found it superfluous caution to keep watch over Joseph, for he could see no wrong in him, and he observed that God was with him, in good days and in bad. He even appointed him to be the overseer of the prison, and as Joseph commanded, so the other prisoners were obliged to do.

Sometime later—the Bible does not say how much time has passed—the king of Egypt becomes angry with his chief cupbearer and his chief baker and banishes them to the same prison where Joseph is being held. The captain of the bodyguard commands Joseph to attend to the new prisoners. It could be that this captain is Potiphar, Joseph's former owner. If so, he knows Joseph's abilities and continues to give him responsibility in spite of his wife's accusation against Joseph.

INTERPRETER OF DREAMS

The cupbearer's responsibilities included bringing Pharaoh his drinks—and possibly taste-testing all his food—and the baker's job included baking Pharaoh's bread. In the course of their duties, the Bible says, each had committed an unspecified offense that enraged the king. Jewish legend says the cupbearer had served wine with a fly in it, and the bread the baker presented contained a small pebble.

One morning in the prison, Joseph finds both men downcast and troubled. Neither man can make sense of his dream from the previous night. Because Egyptians believed that dreams foretold the future, the cupbearer and the baker are extremely interested in their respective dream's meaning. Are they to remain in jail (or worse, be executed), or will they soon be released? Joseph—who has experience with dreams—is immediately interested and says, "Do not interpretations belong to God? Please tell them to me" (Genesis 40:8). (In Qur'an 12:37, Joseph refers to his ability to interpret dreams as "this knowledge the Lord has given me.")

The chief cupbearer tells Joseph that in his dream he saw a vine with three branches, which budded. The buds then ripened into grapes, which the chief cupbearer pressed into Pharaoh's cup; he then placed the cup in Pharaoh's hand. Joseph proceeds to interpret the dream. The three branches, he says, signify three days, which is the time that will pass before the cupbearer is restored to

> Because ancient Egyptians believed dreams were messages from the gods, they often consulted professional interpreters to explain dreams they could not understand.

his office, as symbolized in the dream by his placing the cup in Pharaoh's hand. After relaying the good news, Joseph reveals his own longing to be free once again. He asks a favor from the chief cupbearer: "Only remember me, when it is well with you, and please do me the kindness to mention me to Pharaoh, and so get me out of this house. For I was indeed stolen out of the land of the Hebrews, and here also I have done nothing that they should put me into the pit" (Genesis 40:15).

"So the chief cupbearer told Joseph his dream. He said to him, 'In my dream I saw a vine in front of me, and on the vine were three branches. As soon as it budded, it blossomed, and its clusters ripened into grapes. Pharaoh's cup was in my hand, and I took the grapes, squeezed them into Pharaoh's cup and put the cup in his hand.' 'This is what it means,' Joseph said to him. 'The three branches are three days. Within three days Pharaoh will lift up your head and restore you to your position, and you will put Pharaoh's cup in his hand, just as you used to do when you were his cupbearer'" (Genesis 40:9–13).

Encouraged by Joseph's interpretation of the cupbearer's dream, the chief baker shares his own dream: He had three cake baskets on his head. In the uppermost basket were all sorts of baked foods for Pharaoh, but birds were eating the foods out of the basket. This time, the interpretation Joseph gives is not at all pleasant. He tells the chief baker that the three baskets mean three days, after which Pharaoh will hang him on a tree, where the birds will eat his flesh.

Three days later, both of Joseph's predictions come true. At a birthday celebration for Pharaoh—the only birthday mentioned in the Hebrew Bible—the chief cupbearer is restored to his previous position, and the chief baker is hanged. The last verse of Genesis 40 says, though, that "the chief cupbearer did not remember Joseph, but forgot him."

So Joseph continues to languish in an Egyptian prison for a crime he did not commit. Even so, there is no record in any of the ancient literature—the Bible, the Qur'an, Jewish legend—that Joseph fell into despair or even complained about his situation. Joseph never questions God and never departs from his belief in God, even though he has repeatedly been mistreated—thrown into a pit, sold into slavery, falsely accused, imprisoned, and now completely forgotten. But he never speaks ill of God, and he

---

Joseph is one of only two Hebrew figures from the Old Testament who actually interpret dreams. The other is Daniel. Like Joseph, he stands before a Gentile king and gives credit to God for his interpretation (Daniel 2:28).

continues to believe that God is working for a good greater than he can currently understand. Several years later, Joseph will express this overarching belief when he tells his brothers in Genesis 50:20, "You meant it for evil, but God meant it for good."

The theme that God works for a larger purpose through the lives of individuals runs through the book of Genesis. Joseph is no exception. Just as Joseph's being sold to Potiphar furthers God's purpose, so too does his being forgotten by the royal cupbearer. As one scholar notes, "It became clear that in keeping him in bondage during these two weary years [before he is released], God was doing for him the best thing possible, because the upshot was infinitely more in his favour than anything which the chief butler could have secured if he had remembered him."

THE KING BECKONS

The account picks up again two long years later. Presumably, nothing has changed. The cupbearer has not suddenly remembered Joseph, and Potiphar's wife has not experienced an attack of conscience, so Joseph remains in prison. Once again, however, dreams are about to change the trajectory of Joseph's life.

Pharaoh has dreamed twice in one night. In his first dream, the king is standing by the Nile, the river that was central to Egyptian life, when seven attractive and plump cows walk up out of the water and begin feeding. Seven ugly and thin cows follow, and they proceed to eat the group of seven plump cows. Pharaoh wakes up, then falls back asleep and dreams again. This time, he witnesses seven plump and good ears of grain growing on a single stalk. Suddenly, seven thin and blighted ears of grain sprout and swallow up the good ears.

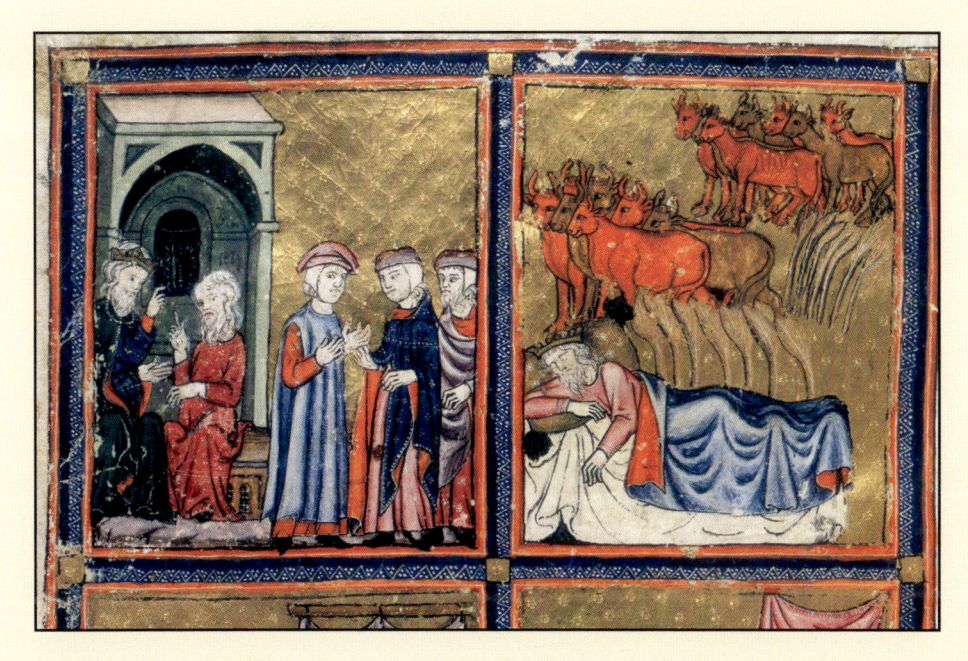

In the left panel of this illustration, Joseph is speaking to Pharaoh and his advisers; the right panel depicts the Egyptian ruler's dream of the seven healthy cows and seven thin cows. Detail from an illuminated manuscript, circa 1300.

The next morning, troubled by his dreams, Pharaoh sends for all the magicians and wise men of Egypt. These would have been men who knew the ancient texts and were adept at interpreting signs—essentially the soothsayers and astrologers of the day. When Pharaoh explains his dreams, however, no one can interpret them. At this point, the chief cupbearer's memory is jogged by his similar situation, and he recounts for Pharaoh how a young Hebrew slave had correctly interpreted both his dream and the chief baker's dream.

Intrigued, Pharaoh immediately sends for Joseph. Guards quickly pull him from the dungeon. They allow him to shave (Egyptian men of the day were mostly clean-shaven) and change his clothes before entering Pharaoh's presence.

Pharaoh, surrounded by advisers and seated on an opulent throne, listens to Joseph interpret his dreams.

Pharaoh says to Joseph, "I have had a dream, and there is no one who can interpret it. I have heard it said of you that when you hear a dream you can interpret it" (Genesis 41:15). Joseph replies, "It is not in me; God will give Pharaoh a favorable answer" (Genesis 41:16). As he did with the cupbearer and baker, Joseph humbly and honestly acknowledges the true source of his interpretive power. It does not come from within him, but from God. The Genesis account never says that God speaks audibly to Joseph; however, Joseph recognizes that the insight needed to impart meaning to symbolic dreams can come only from God. Many men would have personally taken credit for their ability to interpret dreams, but Joseph's righteousness probably works to his benefit. In Egyptian culture dreams were viewed as a method by which the gods communicated with men, and it is likely that Pharaoh would have been reassured to hear that the interpretation of his dreams would come from a divine source rather than from a mere man. Because Egyptians also understood dreams to predict and even determine the future, it would be critical that Pharaoh receive a complete and forthright interpretation of his dreams—regardless of how grim that interpretation might be. According to Josephus, Pharaoh tells Joseph, "I desire thee to suppress nothing out of fear, nor to flatter me with lying words, or with what may please me, although the truth should be of a melancholy nature."

After Pharaoh describes his two dreams, Joseph informs him that both have the same meaning. The seven plump cows from the first dream and the seven healthy ears of grain from the second both represent seven years of good crops; the seven lean cows from the first dream and the seven blighted ears of grain from the second represent seven years of famine. "There will come seven years of great plenty throughout all the land of Egypt," Joseph says, "but after them there will arise seven years of famine and all the plenty will be forgotten in the land of Egypt. The famine will consume the land, and the plenty will be unknown in the land by reason of the famine that will follow, for it will be very severe. And the doubling of Pharaoh's dream means that the thing is fixed by God, and God will shortly bring it about" (Genesis 41:29–32). This interpretation impresses Pharaoh.

Joseph then takes advantage of the opportunity to present a strategy for dealing with the coming crisis. He calls upon his experience as both a shepherd in his father's house and a manager of Potiphar's estate to lay out an effective plan. He also gives advice about what sort of man should administer the plan:

> Now therefore let Pharaoh select a discerning and wise man, and set him over the land of Egypt. Let Pharaoh proceed to appoint overseers over the land and take one-fifth of the produce of the land of Egypt during the seven plentiful years. And let them gather all the food of these good years that are coming and store up grain under the authority of Pharaoh for food in the cities, and let them keep it. That food shall be a reserve for the land against the seven years of famine that are to occur in the land of Egypt, so that the land may not perish through the famine. (Genesis 41:33–36)

It might be surmised that Joseph considers himself a good candidate for the position he has described, though the Bible does not say this explicitly. Again, however, divine providence can be discerned in the Genesis account of Joseph's life. If the cupbearer had remembered Joseph earlier and he had been released from prison, Joseph might not have received an audience with Pharaoh. Because Joseph remained in prison, Pharaoh knows where to find him when his talents are needed.

For his part, Joseph never loses his faith in God's protection and providence. He honestly interprets Pharaoh's dreams, placing his fate in the hands of God.

6

FROM SLAVE TO RULER

After interpreting Pharaoh's dreams and offering his advice, Joseph does not have to wait long for the Egyptian king's response. Pharaoh and his officials are pleased by Joseph's proposal for dealing with the coming famine. "Since God has shown you all this, there is none so discerning and wise as you are," Pharaoh tells Joseph. "You shall be over my house, and all my people shall order themselves as you command. Only as regards the throne will I be greater than you. . . . See, I have set you over all the land of Egypt" (Genesis 41:39–41).

Joseph has witnessed another stunning turn of events. In an instant, Pharaoh has elevated him from an imprisoned Hebrew slave to the second most powerful man in all of Egypt, one of the mightiest nations on earth. As vizier, or viceroy, Joseph will govern Egypt on behalf of Pharaoh. Pharaoh recognizes that Joseph's discernment and wisdom come from God—indeed, he cites this as his reason for making Joseph his vizier. If Joseph had not been humble and honest enough at the outset to credit God for his ability to interpret dreams, Pharaoh might not have been as inclined to listen to his advice. He does not personally know the God of Abraham, Isaac, and Jacob, but Pharaoh seems to recognize the wisdom of heeding God's counsel.

Joseph, despite all he has been through, is still only 30. Yet the trust Pharaoh places in him, and Joseph's newly conferred authority, are immense:

> And Pharaoh said to Joseph, "See, I have set you over all the land of Egypt." Then Pharaoh took his signet ring from his hand and put it on Joseph's hand, and clothed him in garments of fine linen and put a gold chain about his neck. And he made him ride in his second chariot. And they called out before him, "Bow the knee!" Thus he set him over all the land of Egypt. Moreover, Pharaoh said to Joseph, "I am Pharaoh, and without your consent no one shall lift up hand or foot in all the land of Egypt." (Genesis 41:41–44)

A king's signet ring contained his seal. It would be pressed into the hot wax that was put on official documents, thereby showing that the documents carried the

---

The phrase "seven fat years, seven lean years"—from Joseph's interpretation of Pharaoh's dreams—has entered the Jewish culture to describe a situation when fortunate events occur but are followed by unfortunate happenings.

This painting by the 19th-century English artist Sir Lawrence Alma-Tadema depicts Joseph exercising his duties as Pharaoh's viceroy. He is attended by a scribe, who records Joseph's decrees on papyrus scrolls.

full authority of the king. In giving Joseph his signet ring, Pharaoh is essentially saying that Joseph has the authority to transact all affairs of state on his behalf. He is giving Joseph access to all of Egypt's resources, as well as unlimited discretion on how to use them.

Pharaoh also bestows the outer trappings of success on Joseph. His new wardrobe includes the finest garments Joseph has worn since his brothers ripped his coat of many colors from his body. A gold necklace hangs around his neck, and he rides in the second chariot in the land (Pharaoh's was the first), with men walking before him, calling out for Egyptian citizens to bow down to this one-time Hebrew slave.

According to Jewish legend, Pharaoh calls for a parade to celebrate Joseph's ascendance. And what a parade it is:

> Musicians, no less than a thousand striking cymbals and a thousand blowing flutes, and five thousand men with drawn swords gleaming in the air formed the vanguard. Twenty thousand of the king's grandees girt with gold-embroidered leather belts marched at the right of Joseph, and as many at the left of him. The women and the maidens of the nobility looked out of the windows to gaze upon Joseph's beauty, and they poured down chains upon him, and rings and jewels. . . . Servants of the king, preceding him and following him, burnt incense upon his path, and cassia, and all manner of sweet spices, and strewed myrrh and aloes wherever he went.

Jewish legend also has Pharaoh giving Joseph fields and vineyards as a present, in addition to 3,000 talents of silver, 1,000 talents of gold, and onyx stones and many other costly items. Pharaoh also provides Joseph with 100 slaves, and he acquires many more himself. He lives in a magnificent palace that takes three years to build.

One of the most striking aspects in all the accounts is how, in the space of a single day, Joseph's entire life is turned upside down—for the better. As a Jewish rabbi writes, "In the rabbinic *midrash* there is an expression which has provided solace to suffering Jews for thousands of years: 'Salvation can come in the twinkling of an eye.' Joseph wakes up one morning, as he had for the preceding two years, as a falsely accused prisoner in an Egyptian jail. He goes to sleep that night, second in power only to

Pharaoh; truly, Joseph's salvation comes 'in the twinkling of an eye.'"

Another scholar echoes that idea while also emphasizing the role divine providence has played in Joseph's rise:

> Never had there been so sudden a change from dungeon to a chair of state, from absolute slavery to dominion over an empire. And Joseph might now see quite plainly that all his trials, all his unjust treatment, all his shameful experience of evil, were necessary links, divinely planned, in the chain of his advancement. If he had not been sold into Egypt, if he had not been sentenced to the dungeon, if the chief butler had not forgotten him, if he had not been still a prisoner when Pharaoh dreamt his dream, he would not have been called before him, nor have had the opportunity to reveal what was about to happen.

JOSEPH AND ASENATH

The Bible also records that Pharaoh, employing a practice commonly used with foreigners, gives Joseph a new Egyptian name: Zaphenath-paneah, which means either "God speaks, he lives," or "The Nourisher of the Two Lands, the Living One." In addition to the new name, Pharaoh also blesses Joseph with a wife named Asenath, who is the daughter of Potiphera, priest of On. Some sources—including the Jewish historian Josephus and other Jewish legends—suggest this Potiphera is the same Potiphar whose household Joseph once managed.

Other sources consider it more likely that Potiphera—also known as Pentephres—is a different man altogether. On, later renamed Heliopolis by the Greeks, was a city northwest of modern-day Cairo. On functioned as the center of sun worship in ancient Egypt; the temple of the sun god Re was the most important location in the city. The high priest of On was influential in Egyptian religious life. The Bible does not say whether Joseph's father-in-law was the high priest, but it is certainly a possibility, given Joseph's prominence and the need to find a suitable wife for him.

The apocryphal Jewish story of Joseph and Asenath elaborates upon their meeting and courtship and spells out the difficulties inherent in the marriage of two people from different races and cultures. Asenath is an extraordinarily beautiful virgin who makes a habit of secluding herself in her home to avoid potential suitors. The story goes that Joseph is touring the country and plans to dine with Pentephres, who suggests to his daughter that Joseph might make a good husband. She refuses to consider this possibility. When Joseph arrives, however, she is so attracted by his beauty that she falls in love with him. But Joseph rejects her, declaring, "It is not proper for a man who worships God, who blesses with his mouth the living God . . . to kiss a strange woman,

The ancient Egyptians believed obelisks like this one represented the sun god Re. It is possible that Joseph's wife, Asenath, was the daughter of an important member of the cult of Re—perhaps even the high priest.

who blesses with her mouth dead and dumb idols" (Joseph and Asenath 8:5). After the passage of some time, Asenath repents of her idol worship and turns to the God of Joseph and his forefathers. Pharaoh then marries the two in the midst of a celebration.

The story of Joseph and Asenath—and indeed, the overall narrative of Joseph's life—contains a theme that recurs frequently throughout the Old Testament: a Jew succeeding in a country outside his own while remaining true to his Jewish beliefs and customs. Joseph's outward success is undeniable and hardly bears repeating; it suffices to note that he becomes the second most powerful person in one of the ancient world's most powerful empires.

The centrality of Joseph's faith is perhaps not quite so obvious from the Genesis account. The Bible does not record any specific prayers that Joseph prayed to God. Nor does God speak directly to Joseph (as God does to his forefathers or later to Moses). Yet a careful reading of the Genesis narrative yields evidence of Joseph's steadfast faith. For example, Joseph honors God in choosing names for the two sons he and Asenath have together. He names the first son Manasseh ("making to forget"), saying, "God has made me forget all my hardship and all my father's house" (Genesis 41:51). He names his second son Ephraim ("making fruitful"), saying, "For God has made me fruitful in the land of my affliction" (Genesis 41:52). The ending of the name Ephraim is even plural in Hebrew—Joseph is emphasizing the abundance of his blessings.

JOSEPH IN CHARGE

As Joseph is starting his family, he is also beginning his career as vizier of Egypt. He quickly demonstrates his ability. His interpretation of Pharaoh's dream proves valid—during his first seven years as ruler, the earth produces "abundantly" (Genesis 41:47). Joseph takes the skills he has learned as a manager of flocks, households, and prisons and applies them on a much grander scale to an entire country.

Joseph travels frequently throughout Egypt (which was about the size of Texas and New Mexico together), providing direction for the gathering and storage of one-fifth of all the grain grown in the country over the seven years of good harvests. He has each city build a huge granary for storing the surplus grain from the surrounding fields. This simple arrangement will ensure the efficient distribution of grain once the bad harvests begin.

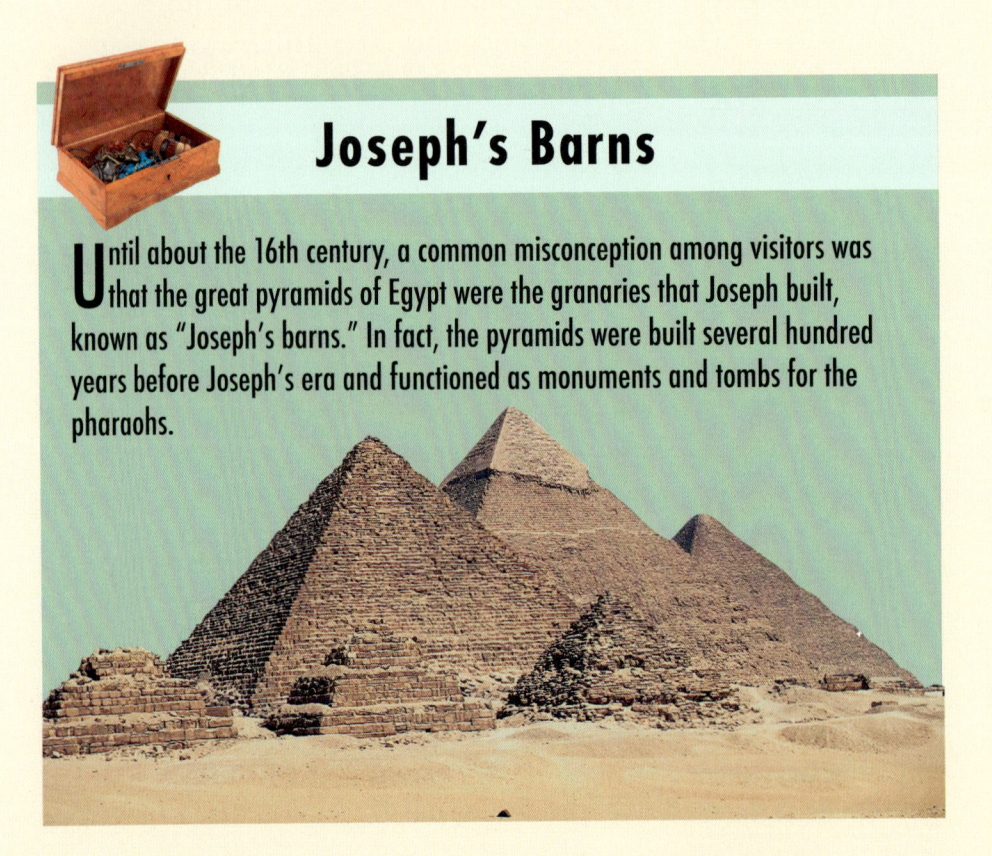

Joseph's Barns

Until about the 16th century, a common misconception among visitors was that the great pyramids of Egypt were the granaries that Joseph built, known as "Joseph's barns." In fact, the pyramids were built several hundred years before Joseph's era and functioned as monuments and tombs for the pharaohs.

"When the famine had spread over all the land, Joseph opened all the storehouses and sold to the Egyptians" (Genesis 41:56). Detail from a Byzantine mosaic, which ornaments a church in Venice, Italy.

The grain produced during those seven good years surpasses anything Egypt has ever seen before. Jewish legend holds that a single ear would produce two heaps of grain. The Bible says, "And Joseph stored up grain in great abundance, like the sand of the sea, until he ceased to measure it, for it could not be measured" (Genesis 41:49).

FAMINE

But as Joseph had predicted, the seven years of plenty come to an end and the seven years of failed harvests begin. Famine was no ordinary occurrence in Egypt. The Nile River generally flooded its banks—and thereby deposited a rich layer of soil in which Egyptian farmers grew their crops—each year. In rare instances, however, an extended drought in the upper regions of the Nile

Egyptian Record-keeping

Scribes would have kept Joseph's grain distribution records on papyrus, one of the earliest forms of paper. The paper was made from the pith of the papyrus plant, a common Egyptian reed.

Hieroglyphics written on a papyrus scroll.

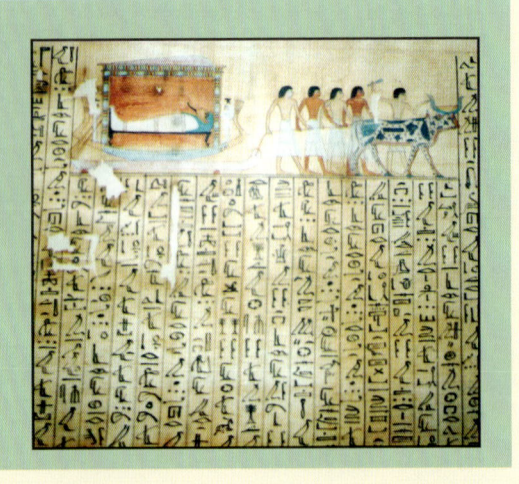

prevented this annual flooding. In hot, arid Egypt, the soil along the Nile would soon be depleted of its nutrients and blasted into hardpan by the blazing sun. Crops would wither and die, and people would soon begin to starve.

Historians tell of one such famine, which devastated Egypt in the 12th century C.E. Eyewitnesses recounted terrible details: "The poor ate carrion, corpses and dogs. . . . As for the number of the poor who perished from hunger and exhaustion, God alone knows what it was. . . . A traveller often passed through a large village without seeing a single inhabitant. . . . The road between Syria and Egypt was like a vast field sown with human bodies."

Joseph's foresight, judgment, and talent save Egypt from this kind of disaster:

> There was famine in all lands, but in all the land of Egypt there was bread. When all the land of Egypt was famished, the people cried to Pharaoh for bread. Pharaoh said to all the Egyptians, "Go to Joseph. What he says to you, do." So when the

famine had spread over all the land, Joseph opened all the storehouses and sold to the Egyptians, for the famine was severe in the land of Egypt. (Genesis 41:54–56)

But it is not only Egyptians who benefit from Joseph's extraordinary work as Pharaoh's vizier. Severe famine has spread well beyond Egypt's borders, and "all the earth came to Egypt to Joseph to buy grain" (Genesis 41:57). Joseph does not turn these desperate people away, showing that he is not only wise but also compassionate.

Josephus attributes Joseph's willingness to help people of any nationality to his sense of the brotherhood of man: "Nor did he open this market of [grain] for the people of that country only, but strangers had liberty to buy also, Joseph being willing that all men, who are naturally akin to one another, should have assistance from those that lived in happiness."

It is against this backdrop that Joseph's brothers reemerge. The famine has reached Canaan and they desperately need food. Their quest to get grain will lead them to the biggest surprise of their lives.

ered how they were doing, what they were like, if his
The Brothers Return

The first verses of Genesis 42 switch the focus back to Jacob and his sons in Canaan. It has been 22 years since Joseph has seen or heard from his family. During that time, he must have occasionally wondered how they were doing, what they were like, if his father was even still alive. The famine has been going on for two years, and Joseph is responsible for distributing stockpiled grain to the people who come to Egypt to buy it. According to Jewish legend, he watches for any sign of Israelite men from Canaan. He requires all those who buy grain to give their names, so that he might locate his family if they show up.

Neither the Bible, nor the Qur'an, nor Jewish legends record any attempt by Joseph to contact his family after his rise to power in Egypt. No explanation for this is offered; it seems likely that Joseph would at least have wanted to let his father know he was still alive. In any case, Jacob and his family have survived through the first two years of the famine but are now running out of grain. His sons appear paralyzed about what to do, but Jacob has heard of the plentiful stores in Egypt, so he sends them to buy grain for the entire clan. He does not send Benjamin, his youngest son and Joseph's full brother, who by this time is at least in his twenties. Jacob fears that harm could befall Benjamin, as it had to Joseph so many years before. Jacob has not forgotten his favorite son—the memory of Joseph continues to color his father's actions even decades later.

FULFILLMENT OF A DREAM

So Reuben, Simeon, Levi, Judah, Dan, Naphtali, Gad, Asher, Issachar, and Zebulun set off for the land of Egypt. Arriving before Joseph, the Egyptian official responsible for grain distribution, they "bowed themselves before him with their faces to the ground . . . and Joseph recognized his brothers, but they did not recognize him. And Joseph remembered the dreams that he had dreamed of them" (Genesis 42:6–9). This is a transcendent moment for Joseph. What he dreamed more than two decades before has come true: his brothers are bowing down before him, just as their sheaves of grain had bowed down to his sheaf of grain in the dream.

That Jacob's sons would not recognize their younger brother now is hardly surprising. So much time has passed, and Joseph speaks the Egyptian tongue and is dressed like an Egyptian. The brothers have no reason to think he is anything other than the Egyptian ruler in charge of handing out grain.

For his part, Joseph wants to find out more about his brothers, so he begins to question them. His tone is accusatory. "And he said to them, 'You are spies, you have come to see the nakedness of the land'" (Genesis 42:9).

His brothers deny this, saying they are honest men (a questionable self-assessment) who have come to Egypt to get grain. But Joseph persists in his accusations, and in defending themselves the brothers reveal more information. They are brothers—10 of the 12 sons of a man in Canaan. Their youngest brother has remained with their father, they say, and the other brother "is no more" (Genesis 42:13). Joseph continues to accuse them of spying, and he says that the only way for them to prove their truthfulness is to bring their youngest brother to Egypt. He deposits them all in jail together for three days.

Various writers have attempted to explain Joseph's apparently harsh behavior toward his brothers at this point in the narrative. According to Philo of Alexandria, a noted Jewish philosopher who lived from the late first century B.C.E. to the early first century C.E., "It was not God's will to reveal the truth as yet, for cogent reasons which were best at the time kept secret . . . [Joseph] forcibly dominated his feelings and, keeping them under the management of his soul, with a carefully considered purpose, he pretended . . . to be hostile and annoyed." Josephus suggests that in concealing his identity, Joseph is trying to glean more information from his brothers about his father and Benjamin. Another interpretation is that Joseph has quickly conceived a plan by which he can test his brothers, to see whether their hearts are still as hard as they were in previous years.

One thing is certain: Joseph has no interest in vengeance. His brothers are completely at his mercy now, yet he does nothing to harm them.

After the brothers have been locked up for three days, Joseph has them brought before him. He tells them they may go home, with supplies of grain, on two conditions: They must promise to return with their youngest brother,

The Brothers Return

"And at this crisis, [Jacob] sent ten of his sons to buy food.... And they, when they had arrived in Egypt, met their brother as if he were a stranger, and being amazed at the dignity with which they beheld him surrounded, they addressed him with prostration according to the ancient fashion, the dreams [of Joseph] now receiving confirmation and fulfillment," wrote the ancient Jewish philosopher Philo of Alexandria.

> Joseph's accusation of spying would have caused his brothers intense fear. Egypt was most vulnerable to invasion from the northern side of the country (where Canaan was located), so Egyptian officials were always on the lookout for spies from that area.

and one of them must remain behind as a prisoner, serving as surety that they will keep this promise. "Do this and you will live, for I fear God," Joseph says (Genesis 42:18).

The brothers agree to the plan. While still in the same room as Joseph, they begin to discuss what is at the back of each man's mind: their treatment of Joseph 22 years before. "They said to one another, 'In truth, we are guilty concerning our brother, in that we saw the distress of his soul, when he begged us and we did not listen. That is why this distress has come upon us'" (Genesis 42:21). Reuben, who has begun to fear for their lives, is more direct. "Did I not tell you," he asks, "not to sin against the boy? But you did not listen. So now there comes a reckoning for his blood" (Genesis 42:22). In the original Hebrew, "reckoning" literally means a payment of death.

As they talk about this painful subject, the brothers do not realize that the ruler standing before them—who has used an interpreter in all their dealings thus far—understands Hebrew and is, in fact, the long-lost brother about whom they are speaking. Joseph hears the entire discussion and is overcome with emotion. He leaves the room and weeps. After regaining his composure, he returns and orders Simeon bound and taken away. The text does not say why Joseph chooses to keep Simeon rather than Reuben, the firstborn, as his captive. The reason might be that whereas Reuben had attempted to thwart the brothers' plans to sell Joseph into slavery two decades earlier, Simeon had been one of the instigators of that vile act.

In any event, Joseph orders his servants to fill the brothers' grain bags and to give them provisions for the trip home. Without the brothers' knowledge, he also orders that the money they have paid for the grain be put back into their bags. On the way home, one of the brothers opens his sack to feed his donkey and discovers the bundle of money there. Instead of rejoicing at their good fortune, the brothers—who are afflicted with guilty consciences—look for a darker meaning. "At this their hearts failed them," Genesis 42:28 says, "and they turned trembling to one another, saying, 'What is this that God has done to us?'"

DEBATING AT HOME

Once home, the nine brothers relate their story—including the Egyptian ruler's demand to see Benjamin upon their return—to their father. As they unload their sacks of grain, they discover that each man's money has been returned. Again, they are all afraid. Jacob takes an especially pessimistic view of the situation. "You have bereaved me of my children," he says. "Joseph is no more, and Simeon is no more, and now you would take Benjamin. All this has come against me" (Genesis 42:36). Even though Benjamin is by now grown and possibly has a family of his own, Jacob is determined not to send him to Egypt for fear that he will lose his only other son by Rachel. Reuben offers the lives of his two sons to his father as a guarantee against Benjamin's life, but Jacob will have none of it. "My son shall not go down with you, for his brother is dead and he is the only one left. If harm should happen to him on the journey that you are to make, you would bring down

Egypt and Canaan in the Time of Joseph

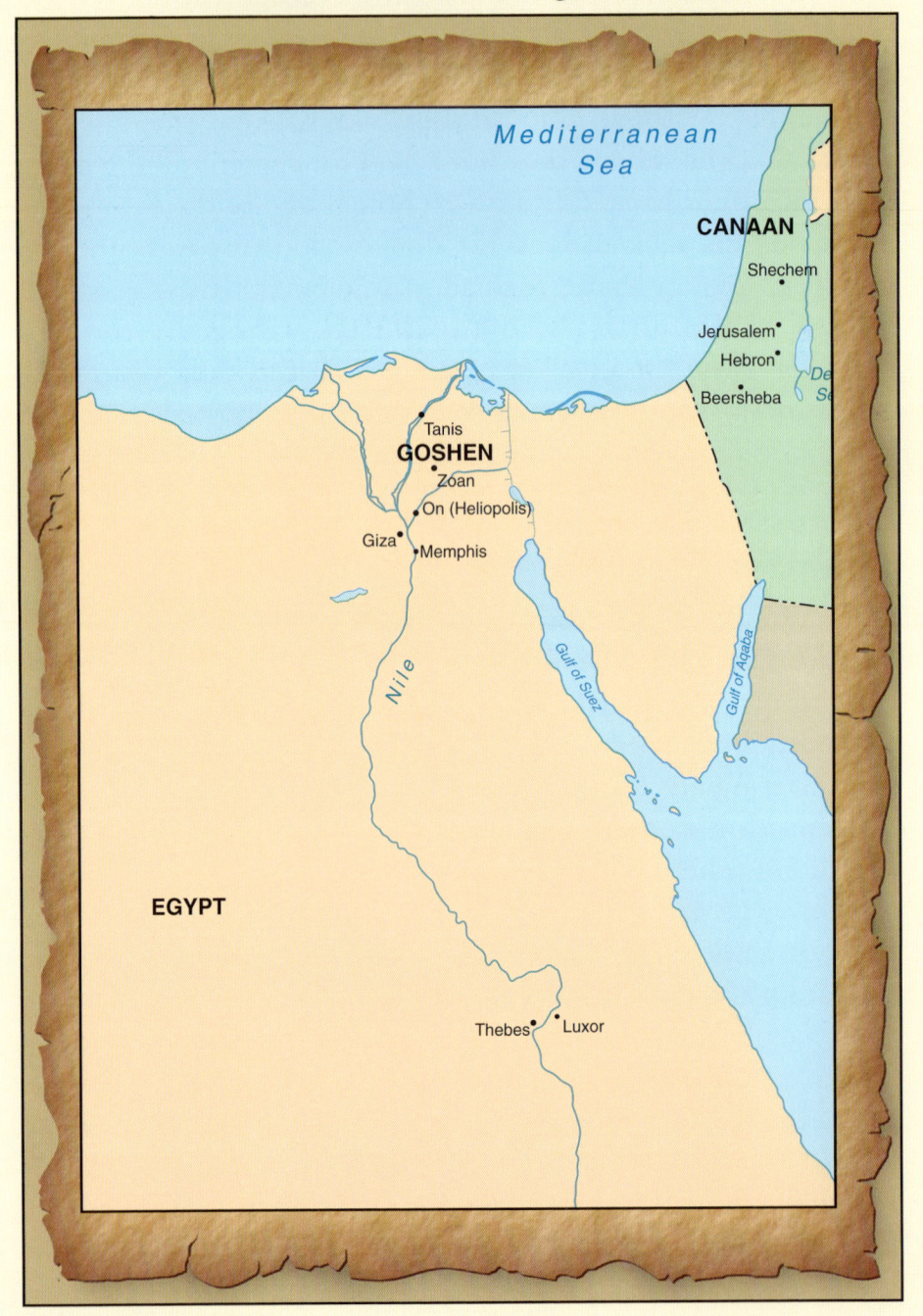

my gray hairs with sorrow to Sheol [the place of the dead]" (Genesis 42:38).

But the famine continues just as severely as before, and the grain the brothers have bought in Egypt eventually begins to run out. Jacob tells the brothers to go to Egypt again and buy more grain, making no mention of sending Benjamin. Judah reminds him of the necessity that Benjamin accompany them: "The man solemnly warned us, saying, 'You shall not see my face unless your brother is with you.' If you will send our brother with us, we will go down and buy you food. But if you will not send him, we will not go down, for the man said to us, 'You shall not see my face unless your brother is with you'" (Genesis 43:3–5). Jacob asks his sons how they could have treated him so badly by telling the Egyptian ruler about Benjamin. The brothers reasonably reply that there was no way they could have known he would require them to bring Benjamin to Egypt. Judah finally makes an appeal that breaks through Jacob's defenses: "Send the boy with me, and we will arise and go, that we may live and not die, both we and also our little ones. I will be a pledge of his safety. From my hand you shall require him. If I do not bring him back to you and set him before you, then let me bear the blame forever" (Genesis 43:8–9). In his argument, Judah points out one inescapable fact—if they do not obtain food from Egypt, they and their families will die. It is that simple.

Jacob realizes that "it must be so" and tells the brothers to carry gifts to the Egyptian lord, including "a little balm and a little honey, gum, myrrh, pistachio nuts, and almonds" (Genesis 43:11). These items—some of which are still presented as gifts today—were plentiful in Canaan but relatively scarce in Egypt. Gifts had helped Jacob defuse a tense situation before (with his brother Esau), and he is hoping they will have a good influence in this situation as well. He also tells his sons to take double the usual amount of money with them so they can return what they found in their sacks after the first trip. In his parting speech, he asks God to bless the endeavor, but he also sounds a note of resignation: "May God Almighty grant you mercy before the man, and may he send back your other brother and Benjamin. And as for me, if I am bereaved of my children, I am bereaved" (Genesis 43:14).

And so the brothers, now with Benjamin in tow, set off for Egypt bearing presents, money, and guilty consciences. Soon they will be forced to confront the legacy of their long-ago betrayal of Joseph.

BEFORE JOSEPH

After the brothers arrive in Egypt, Joseph spots them approaching, and he sees that Benjamin is among them. Joseph tells the steward of his house (Jewish legend says the steward is his own son Manasseh) to "bring the men into the house, and slaughter an animal and make ready, for the men are to dine with me at noon" (Genesis 43:16). This request must have seemed odd—Joseph certainly would not have had a special meal prepared every time foreigners arrived to buy grain—but the steward does as he is told.

When they realize they are about to enter the Egyptian official's personal dwelling, the brothers become afraid. They assume he is angry about the money they found in their sacks and that he will force them to become his slaves. They worriedly explain the situation to the steward, concluding their explanation by saying, "So we have brought it again with us, and we have brought other money down with us to buy food. We do not know who put the money in our sacks" (Genesis 43:22). The steward tells them not to be afraid. "Your God and the God of your father has put treasure in your sacks for you," he says (Genesis 43:23). The steward also brings Simeon out to join his brothers.

When Joseph arrives for the meal, his brothers give him their gifts and bow before him (Joseph's dream is once again coming true). He asks if their father is still alive, and they assure him that he is. Then, looking at Benjamin—his mother's son, his only full brother—Joseph asks, "Is this your youngest brother, of whom you spoke to me? God be gracious to you, my son!" (Genesis 43:29). At this point Joseph is overcome with emotion and hurries out of the room. He reaches his bedroom before breaking down and weeping.

After regaining his composure, Joseph returns and orders that the meal be served. As the ruler, he sits by himself. The Egyptians present are seated at another table. (Because cows were sacred in their culture, Egyptians considered eating meals with Hebrews, who did eat beef, an abomination.) The brothers are all seated together at their own table in front of Joseph. When they come to the table, the men look at one another in amazement—Joseph has seated all 11 brothers in correct age order, from Reuben the oldest down to Benjamin the youngest. He sends food from his table to theirs, giving Benjamin a much larger portion than the rest of the brothers. Philo explains that Joseph "entertained his mother's son on a richer scale than the rest, but meanwhile observed each of them to judge from their looks whether they still kept some secret envy." For their part, the brothers—who must have felt their fear draining away—"drank and were merry with him" (Genesis 43:34).

JOSEPH REVEALED

Joseph senses that his brothers are changed men, but he wants to give them one more test before revealing his identity to them. In Jewish tradition, the classic test of whether someone has truly repented is to put that person in the same situation that led to previous wrongdoing and see whether he or she behaves differently. So Joseph devises a plan that will place one of the brothers in peril, to see whether the others will respond by defending him or abandoning him (as had happened to Joseph when the brothers sold him into slavery).

THE FINAL TEST

The morning after their meal with Joseph, the brothers rise early to leave for home. Unbeknownst to them, Joseph has instructed his steward not only to fill the men's sacks with grain but also, once again, to return the money they have used to purchase grain and to put his royal silver cup in Benjamin's sack. This cup is mentioned later as being used for divination, which does not necessarily mean Joseph practiced that ancient art common to the Egyptians; the cup, however, is a tangible symbol of the authority of Joseph's office. Taking it would be a serious crime.

Soon after his brothers depart, Joseph orders his steward to catch up to them and ask, "Why have you repaid evil for good? Is it not from this that my lord drinks, and by this that he practices divination? You have done evil in doing this" (Genesis 44:4–5).

When the steward overtakes the brothers, he repeats the accusation. The men proclaim their innocence and note that they have been so conscientious as to attempt to return the money found in their sacks after their first trip to Egypt. They even offer to pay a steep price if the steward finds the cup in any of the sacks. "Whichever of your servants is found with it shall die, and we also will be my lord's servants," they say (Genesis 44:9). The steward accepts a less severe proposal, saying, "Let it be as you

"Now Joseph gave these instructions to the steward of his house: 'Fill the men's sacks with as much food as they can carry, and put each man's silver in the mouth of his sack. Then put my cup, the silver one, in the mouth of the youngest one's sack, along with the silver for his grain.' And he did as Joseph said"

say: he who is found with it shall be my servant, and the rest shall be innocent" (Genesis 44:10).

The steward searches the brothers' bags. When he finds the cup in Benjamin's sack, the other brothers tear their clothes in grief and anguish. Their father's worst fears are being realized; Benjamin is sure to be held in Egypt. The brothers reload their donkeys, and everyone returns to the city to face Joseph once again.

When the brothers arrive back at Joseph's house, he asks them, "What deed is this that you have done? Do you not know that a man like me can indeed practice divination?" (Genesis 44:15)—implying that he knew they had taken the cup. Judah, who has emerged as the brothers' leader and spokesman, responds by asking rhetorically whether there is any way the brothers can clear themselves—he knows there is not—and then he makes an interesting statement applying not just to the cup, but to the brothers' treachery more than 20 years before: "God has found out the guilt of your servants" (Genesis 44:16). The work on the brothers' consciences is complete—they recognize their sin and are determined to change, as Joseph will find out momentarily. Judah tells Joseph that all the brothers will be his servants, but Joseph replies that it is only necessary that Benjamin remain. The rest are free to return to their father.

This sets up one of the most dramatic and moving scenes in the Old Testament. Desperate at the thought of his father's grief if Benjamin does not return home, Judah approaches Joseph and delivers one of the longest recorded speeches in the Torah:

> Oh, my lord, please let your servant speak a word in my lord's ears, and let not your anger burn against your servant, for you are like Pharaoh him-

self. My lord asked his servants, saying, "Have you a father, or a brother?" And we said to my lord, "We have a father, an old man, and a young brother, the child of his old age. His brother is dead, and he alone is left of his mother's children, and his father loves him." Then you said to your servants, "Bring him down to me, that I may set my eyes on him." We said to my lord, "The boy cannot leave his father, for if he should leave his father, his father would die." Then you said to your servants, "Unless your youngest brother comes down with you, you shall not see my face again."

When we went back to your servant my father, we told him the words of my lord. And when our father said, "Go again, buy us a little food," we said, "We cannot go down. If our youngest brother goes with us, then we will go down. For we cannot see the man's face unless our youngest brother is with us." Then your servant my father said to us, "You know that my wife bore me two sons. One left me, and I said, Surely he has been torn to pieces, and I have never seen him since. If you take this one also from me, and harm happens to him, you will bring down my gray hairs in evil to Sheol."

Now therefore, as soon as I come to your servant my father, and the boy is not with us, then, as his life is bound up in the boy's life, as soon as he sees that the boy is not with us, he will die, and your servants will bring down the gray hairs of your servant our father with sorrow to Sheol. For your servant became a pledge of safety for the boy to my father, saying, "If I do not bring him back to you, then I shall bear the blame before my father all my life." Now therefore, please let your servant remain instead of the boy as a servant to my lord, and let the boy go back with his brothers. For how can I go back to my father if the boy is not with me? I fear to see the evil that would find my father. (Genesis 44:18–34)

Revealed

Joseph is dumbfounded by Judah's plea. He sees exactly how much Judah's heart—and the hearts of his brothers—has changed in 20 years. No longer is Judah scheming to sell a brother to slave traders; instead, he is begging to be allowed to endure the punishment that belongs to another brother. Rather than deceiving his father, he now feels compassion for Jacob. His words, "For how can I go back to my father if the boy is not with me?" demonstrate clearly that his biggest concern is not himself, but his father. Judah and his brothers have become honorable men, worthy of carrying the mantle of leaders of the nation of Israel. (For Christians, Judah's words and sacrificial actions even call to mind the ultimate sacrifice of Jesus Christ many centuries later; Jesus was a Jew whose lineage could be traced back to the tribe of Judah, son of Jacob.)

Rabbi Telushkin points out the significance and meaning of Judah's words: "In the thousands of years since the Torah was given, Judah's actions have served as the prototype of true repentance. . . . The twelfth-century philosopher Moses Maimonides notes that full repentance only comes about when a person is subjected to the same situation in which he once sinned, and does so no more. . . . Judah's noble offer convinces Joseph that his test has gone far enough; because his brothers have truly changed, he can now reveal himself."

Genesis says that after Judah's speech, "Joseph could not control himself" (Genesis 45:1). He orders everyone except his brothers out of the room and weeps so loudly that even those who have left the room can hear him. In the midst of his tears, he proclaims, "I am Joseph! Is my father still alive?" (Genesis 45:3).

Joseph's brothers are dumbstruck. Beckoning them to come closer to him, Joseph continues:

I am your brother, Joseph, whom you sold into Egypt. And now do not be distressed or angry with yourselves because you sold me here, for *God sent me before you to preserve life*. For the famine has been in the land these two years, and there are yet five years in which there will be neither plowing nor harvest. *And God sent me before you to preserve for you a remnant on earth*, and *to keep alive for you many survivors*. So it was not you who sent me here, but God. He has made me a father to Pharaoh, and lord of all his house and ruler over all the land of Egypt. (Genesis 45:4–8, emphasis added)

Joseph reveals himself to his astonished brothers. This 18th-century painting is by the French artist Charles Thévenin.

> The description of Joseph's reconciliation with his brothers has touched countless people over the centuries. In 1960 Pope John XXIII, the head of the Roman Catholic Church, greeted world Jewish leaders at an interfaith meeting with the words "I am Joseph your brother."

In just a few words, Joseph shows his brothers the power of forgiveness. He harbors no anger or bitterness toward them—in fact, he has come to see that, painful though the incident was, his sale into slavery has served God's greater purpose. It brought Joseph to Egypt, where he eventually found himself in a position to interpret Pharaoh's dream, which in turn led to his appointment as vizier, which in turn allowed him to take the necessary measures to gather enough grain to sustain people—including his family—through the coming famine. Thus if Joseph's brothers had not sold him into slavery, Jacob and all his family would have perished. God's promise to make Abraham's descendants as numerous as the sand of the seashore and the stars of the sky could not have been fulfilled.

In the Qur'an, the brothers explicitly admit their guilt: "'By the Lord,' they said. 'God has exalted you above all. We have indeed done wrong'" (Qur'an 12:91). But, as in the Bible narrative, Joseph does not want them to continue dwelling on the guilt and shame they have carried for so long. "None shall reproach you this day," he says. "May God forgive you: of all those that show mercy He is the most merciful" (Qur'an 12:92).

According to Josephus, Joseph comforts his brothers by pointing them to the ultimate outcome of their actions, rather than the immediate result: "Do not, therefore, let your evil intentions when you condemned me, and that bitter remorse which might follow, be a grief to you now, because those intentions were frustrated. Go, therefore, your way, rejoicing in what has happened by the divine providence, and inform your father of it."

The brothers, who have received the greatest shock of their lives, accept Joseph's freely offered forgiveness. Amid an abundance of weeping, Joseph and his brothers talk and reconcile. In his testament, Simeon explains how Joseph could still love even a brother who had wanted to kill him: "Now Joseph was a good man, and had the Spirit of God within him: being compassionate and pitiful, he bore no malice against me; but loved me even as the rest of his brethren" (Simeon 2:4).

THE BROTHERS RETURN TO JACOB

As joyful as the reunion is, Joseph longs to see his father—and to provide for Jacob and his family during the remaining years of the famine. He says to his brothers:

> Hurry and go up to my father and say to him, "Thus says your son Joseph, God has made me lord of all Egypt. Come down to me; do not tarry. You shall dwell in the land of Goshen, and you shall be near me, you and your children and your children's children, and your flocks, your herds, and all that you have. There I will provide for you, for there are yet five years of famine to come, so that you and your household, and all that you have, do not come to poverty." (Genesis 45:9–11)

When Pharaoh hears the news of Joseph's reunion with his brothers, he is pleased. He orders that Egyptian wagons be sent back to Canaan with Joseph's brothers, so they will have room to bring to Egypt their wives, children, and entire households. Pharaoh also promises to give Joseph's relatives the best land in Egypt on which to settle. All this must be read as a mark of the extremely high regard in which Pharaoh holds Joseph. The former slave has served Egypt so honestly and capably that Pharaoh honors him by providing abundantly for his family.

And so Joseph sends his brothers back to Canaan to retrieve his father and their families. He gives each brother a change of clothes, but to Benjamin he gives five changes of clothes and 300 shekels of silver. To his father he sends 10 donkeys weighed down with the good things of Egypt, and 10 more donkeys loaded with grain, bread, and provisions for the journey. He also gives his brothers one parting piece of advice: "Do not quarrel on the way" (Genesis 45:24). Joseph knows that besides bearing the

Curing Jacob's Blindness

In the Qur'anic version of the story, Joseph's brothers return home from their second trip to Egypt without Benjamin, whom Joseph has accused of stealing his cup. Jacob is so distraught at the loss of Joseph and now Benjamin that "his eyes went white with grief, and he was oppressed with silent sorrow" (Qur'an 12:84).

Jacob sends his remaining sons back to Egypt once again to seek news of their missing brothers (presumably his sons have told him how they earlier sold Joseph into slavery there). This time, Joseph reveals himself and forgives his brothers for their transgression against him. He tells them to take one of his shirts home to throw over Jacob's face. This, Joseph says, will restore their father's sight.

Joseph's remedy for Jacob's blindness does indeed prove successful. Jacob then travels to Egypt to visit his long-lost son.

joyful news that he is alive, his brothers still face the difficult task of informing Jacob of their treachery in selling him into slavery and deceiving their father for so long. He does not want them to make matters worse with recriminations.

When the brothers arrive home and tell their father, "Joseph is still alive and he is ruler over all the land of Egypt," Jacob's heart "became numb, for he did not believe them" (Genesis 45:26). Once the brothers explain all that Joseph had said and Jacob sees the Egyptian wagons that have been sent for him, his spirit revives and he says, "It is enough; Joseph my son is still alive. I will go and see him before I die" (Genesis 45:28).

ISRAELITES IN EGYPT

After Jacob makes the decision to go to Egypt, 70 members of his household, including his sons and their children, gather their livestock and goods, load into Pharaoh's wagons, and begin the journey. On the way, the entourage spends the night in Beersheba, a frequent place of worship for both Abraham and Isaac. Jacob offers sacrifices to the God of his fathers, and that night, God speaks to him in a vision, assuring him that the decision to venture to Egypt is wise. "I am God, the God of your father," he says. "Do not be afraid to go down to Egypt, for there I will make you into a great nation. I myself will go down with you to Egypt, and I will also bring you up again, and Joseph's hand shall close your eyes" (Genesis 46:3–4).

This assurance must have meant a great deal to Jacob. God's previous promises concerning the great nation that would descend from Jacob—the nation of Israel—

have been connected with Canaan. It cannot have been easy for Jacob to leave the Promised Land. In fact, so great is the pull of Canaan on Jacob that, as he is about to die in Egypt, he gets his sons to pledge that they will bury him with his forefathers in Canaan. (Joseph will do the same thing.) Jacob's vision at Beersheba and the promise in it—that God will make a mighty nation through Jacob's line—means that Jacob does not have to worry that he is somehow breaking the covenant God established with Abraham; in fact, Jacob's going down to Egypt is the means by which God has chosen to accomplish his purpose. Jacob specifically hears that his descendants will one day emerge from Egypt and come back to the land he loves. The book of Exodus bears out God's promise to Jacob, as the nation of Israel—grown to some 2 million souls from the original 70—marches out of the land of Egypt 430 years later (Exodus 12:40) to claim the Promised Land of Canaan.

God also promises Jacob at Beersheba that he will have a relationship with his beloved son Joseph. Joseph will be the one to close Jacob's eyes once he has passed away.

JACOB AND JOSEPH REUNITED

Thus renewed in his purpose to immigrate to Egypt, Jacob sends Judah ahead of the group to point the way to Goshen, located in the Egyptian Delta region, where Joseph has decided the family will settle. The geography of the area fits well with the needs of the herds and livestock that Jacob is bringing from Canaan.

As the group draws closer, Joseph cannot wait any longer—he prepares his chariot and hurries to Goshen, where he has an emotional reunion with his father. "He [Joseph] presented himself to him [Jacob] and fell on his neck and wept on his neck a good while. Israel said to Joseph, 'Now let me die, since I have seen your face and know that you are still alive'" (Genesis 46:29–30).

Joseph, who knows the proper Egyptian customs, tells his father and brothers how he plans to install them in the land of Goshen—he will inform Pharaoh ahead of time that his family members are shepherds who have brought their flocks and herds from Canaan. Joseph knows that "every shepherd is an abomination to the Egyptians" (Genesis 46:34), so he wants to keep his family on their own in the land of Goshen, both to protect them and to preserve their identity as Israelites. He takes five men—possibly the five oldest brothers—and presents them to Pharaoh, who asks what their occupations are. They reply, "Your servants are shepherds, as our fathers were" (Genesis 47:3). Then, in keeping with the deference of visitors, they ask permission to live in the land of Goshen: "We have come to sojourn in the land, for there is no pasture for your servant's flocks, for the famine is severe in the land of Canaan. And now, please let your servants dwell in the land of Goshen" (Genesis 47:4). Pharaoh responds with a generous offer that shows his respect for Joseph and fulfills the commitment he has already made: "Your father and your brothers have come to you," he tells Joseph. "The land of Egypt is before you. Settle your father and your brothers in the best of the land. Let them settle in the land of Goshen and if you know any able men among them, put them in charge of my livestock" (Genesis 47:5–6). Pharaoh recognizes that a family that has produced as skilled a manager as Joseph might have other talented individuals who could benefit his kingdom.

Joseph then brings in his father to stand before Pharaoh. Pharaoh inquires how old Jacob is, and he replies in typically pessimistic fashion, "The days of the

Israelites in Egypt 93

This illustrated page from The World Chronicle, *a 14th-century history book published in Germany, shows Jacob and his family during their journey to Egypt (top) and the joyful reunion of Joseph and Jacob.*

This mural from an Egyptian pharaoh's tomb depicts members of a Semitic tribe asking for permission to enter Egypt, just as Jacob's family did. The tribespeople are wearing colorful striped robes and accompanied by their herds of animals.

years of my sojourning are 130 years. Few and evil have been the days of the years of my life, and they have not attained to the days of the years of the life of my fathers in the days of their sojourning" (Genesis 47:9). His response is accurate—his life is shorter than Abraham's and Isaac's, and he has never actually possessed the land of Canaan— but his life is now taking a turn for the better. For the next 17 years, he will enjoy a life of abundance in the best of the land of Egypt. Before he leaves Pharaoh's presence, he blesses the Egyptian ruler, presumably in the name of his God (and not according to Pharaoh's gods).

The official business transacted, Joseph provides food for his family in accord with the number of their dependents and settles them in "the best of the land, in the land of Rameses" (Genesis 47:11). The land of Rameses is the same as the land of Goshen. In other places this land is called Zoan or Tanis, after the cities of the region. It encompassed a fertile area along a branch of the Nile. One ancient Egyptian writer vividly described the richness of the region given to the Israelites:

> Its fields are full of good things, and life passes in constant plenty and abundance. Its canals are rich in fish; its meadows are green with vegetables; there is no end of the lentils; melons with a taste like honey grow in the irrigated fields. Its barns are full of wheat and durra, and reach as high as heaven. Onions and sesame are in the enclosures. . . . The vine and the almond-tree and the fig-tree grow in its gardens. Sweet is their wine for the inhabitants of Keim. They mix it with honey.

THE FAMINE CONTINUES

Joseph may have settled his family in Goshen, but he still has a country to run, and it remains beset by famine.

The mention of Rameses in the story of Joseph is an anachronism. Rameses was the name of several pharaohs of the 19th dynasty, the first of whom did not come to the throne until the late 14th century B.C.E., hundreds of years after Joseph. The mention of Rameses in the story of Joseph is evidence that the text was written much later than the events depicted (Moses is traditionally credited as the author of Genesis).

Genesis 47:13 says there is "no food" in all the land, and Egypt and Canaan are "languishing" because of the famine. It is so severe that the people are not producing any crops—they are forced to buy all of their grain from Pharaoh. The Bible says Joseph gathered up "all the money that was found in the land of Egypt and in the land of Canaan, in exchange for the grain that they bought. And Joseph brought the money into Pharaoh's house" (Genesis 47:13).

Once their money runs out, the Egyptians come to Joseph and ask him to give them food for free. Joseph, ever the fair and innovative businessman, avoids handouts, which would lead to dependency. Instead he says, "Give your livestock and I will give you food in exchange for your livestock, if your money is gone" (Genesis 47:16). This arrangement lasts for a year, and the people trade horses, flocks, herds, and donkeys for food.

The next year, the people come again to Joseph with a new plea, backed by a good argument:

> We will not hide from my lord that our money is all spent. The herds of livestock are my lord's. There is nothing left in the sight of my lord but our bodies and our land. Why should we die before your eyes, both we and our land? Buy us and our land for food, and we with our land will be servants to Pharaoh. And give us seed that we may live and not die, and that the land may not be desolate. (Genesis 47:18–19)

Joseph agrees to the proposal and buys "all the land of Egypt for Pharaoh, for all the Egyptians sold their fields" (Genesis 47:20). The only ones exempt are priests, who live on a fixed allowance from Pharaoh. Joseph gives the people food and seed to sow, and since Pharaoh now owns the land, Joseph enacts a law by which one-fifth of all that the people grow in the future will go to Pharaoh. The people will keep four-fifths as their own so that they will be able to feed their own households. This 20 percent tax given to Pharaoh is the first national income tax recorded in Scripture, and it seems to be a typical tax for that period in history.

In another attempt to help the people endure the devastation of the famine, Joseph also moves parts of the population into various cities in the land ("made servants of them" in Genesis 47:21 literally means "removed them to the cities"). In response to all of Joseph's strategies for

Carving of an Egyptian peasant with a bull, from a temple at Luxor. According to the biblical account, Joseph's strategies during the seven famine years not only save the people, but also enrich Pharaoh by giving him ownership of land and livestock and a share in Egypt's annual agricultural production.

What's in a Number?

In Acts 7:14, Stephen, recounting the story of Joseph, says 75 members of Jacob's household went down to Egypt. The difference of five people (Genesis 46:27 says there are 70 settlers) is explained by the fact that as a Hellenist (a Jew who had adopted Greek culture) Stephen used the Greek translation of the Old Testament, known as the Septuagint. The Septuagint includes in its count five people actually born in the land of Egypt: two sons of Manasseh, two sons of Ephraim, and one grandson of Ephraim.

In both cases, the number of counted people in Jacob's household who go to Egypt does not include servants. If servants moved with Jacob and his sons, the number actually settling in Egypt might be around 3,000 people, based on other recorded numbers of servants in the Bible (Abraham roused 318 servants of his house in his attempt to rescue his nephew Lot in Genesis 14, for example).

---

surviving the famine, the people tell him, "You have saved our lives: may it please my lord, we will be servants to Pharaoh" (Genesis 47:25).

Pharaoh must have been pleased with Joseph's performance. Joseph has managed the country through an extremely harsh period, bringing an incredible quantity of goods, money, and land into the coffers of Egypt. And he has done so with integrity. It would have been easy for him to line his own pockets, but the Bible says he brought all the money into the house of Pharaoh. Joseph's management has also been characterized by compassion: he has used his power not simply to benefit Pharaoh, but to save the lives of many people.

Jacob and his family, meanwhile, flourish in the land of Goshen. They "gained possessions in it, and were fruitful and multiplied greatly," according to Genesis 47:27.

Pharaoh lets them live as they please, and the native Egyptians have no problems with them either. Left alone, the Israelites prosper. Their flocks and goods increase, as do the numbers of their families.

EPHRAIM AND MANASSEH

At this point, the Genesis narrative skips ahead 17 years. Joseph is now 56 years old, and his father is 147. Jacob has experienced 17 blessed years that he never expected, but the time of his death is drawing near. He wants to take care of the last remaining details of his life, so he calls Joseph to his side and extracts a promise that Joseph will not bury him in Egypt, but will carry him to the burial place of his fathers in Canaan. Joseph swears that he will honor his father's dying request.

Soon after this, as Jacob is near death, Joseph brings his two sons, Manasseh and Ephraim, to see their grandfather one last time. Jacob summons his strength, sits up in bed, and briefly recounts the covenant God made with Abraham and repeated to him: "Behold, I will make you fruitful and multiply you, and I will make of you a company of peoples and will give this land [Canaan] to your offspring after you for an everlasting possession" (Genesis 48:4). The covenant attachment to Canaan explains Jacob's dying request to be buried there.

Jacob then uses the formal language of adoption to bequeath an inheritance to Joseph's two sons. "Your two sons . . . are mine; Ephraim and Manasseh shall be mine as Reuben and Simeon are," he says (Genesis 48:5). In effect, Jacob is stripping the double portion of the inheritance reserved for Reuben, the firstborn son, and granting it to Joseph through each of his sons. The first book of Chronicles explains why: "Reuben . . . was the firstborn, but because he defiled his father's couch, his birthright was given to the sons of Joseph the son of Israel, so that he could not be enrolled as the oldest son" (1 Chronicles 5:1). Reuben's punishment for taking his father's concubine for himself (recounted in Genesis 35:22) is to lose his birthright, and Jacob is honest enough to tell him so when he later blesses each of his sons just before he dies. "Reuben, you are my firstborn, my might, and the firstfruits of my strength, preeminent in dignity and preeminent in power," Jacob says. "Unstable as water, you shall not have preeminence, because you went up to your father's bed; then you defiled it" (Genesis 49:3–4).

The outcome of Jacob's decision is that Joseph's place as head of a tribe of Israel is divided between his two sons. When the Israelites return to the land of Canaan more than 400 years later, the land will be divided into 12 territories. The tribe of Levi receives no actual land because they serve as priests to the nation and do not require their own territory. Ephraim and Manasseh make up the difference, keeping the number of tribes at 12.

After Jacob announces that Manasseh and Ephraim will have an equal inheritance with his own sons, he wants to bless them by placing a hand on each boy's head. But by this time Jacob is blind and becomes confused about who the two boys are. (His uncertainty brings to mind the confusion of Isaac, Jacob's father, as Jacob manipulated him into bestowing Esau's firstborn blessing upon him.) After Joseph explains that the boys are his sons, Jacob kisses them and says to Joseph, "I never expected to see your face; and behold, God has let me see your offspring also" (Genesis 48:11). Joseph sends his sons forward in the traditional manner to receive their blessing, with Manasseh (the firstborn) at Jacob's right hand, and Ephraim at Jacob's left hand. Jacob, however, crosses his hands and blesses the boys, asking God to carry his name through

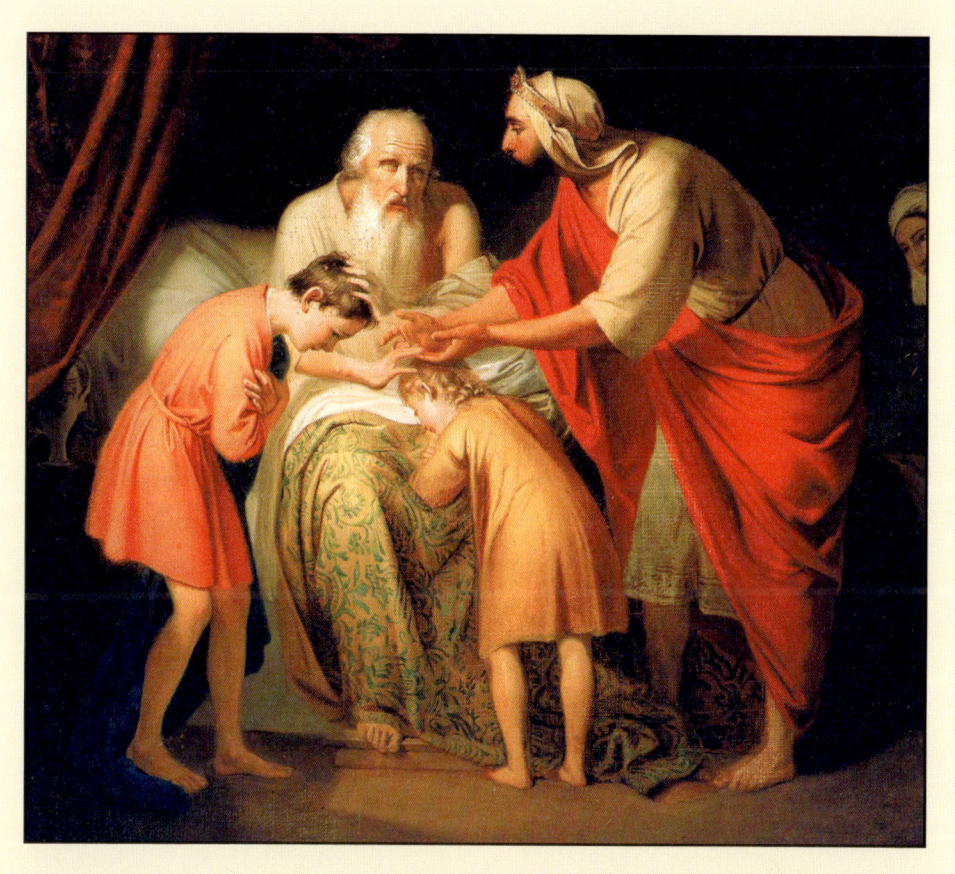

Jacob (seated) blesses his grandsons Ephraim and Manasseh. Joseph's attempt to uncross his father's hands is unsuccessful, so Ephraim receives the blessing that would normally go to the firstborn, Manasseh.

them and let them grow into a multitude on the earth. The biblical text actually says that Jacob blesses Joseph (Genesis 48:15) as he is beginning to bless the boys; the implication is that blessing Joseph's sons, who are his heirs, is the same as blessing Joseph himself. Again the boys have been accorded a standing equal to Jacob's other 11 sons.

Joseph then tries to move Jacob's hands to their correct positions, but Jacob refuses and tells Joseph that his younger son will become greater than his older son—a prophecy that echoes Joseph's own ascent to a higher position than his brothers. Jacob then closes out the blessing with the words, "By you Israel will pronounce blessings, saying, 'God make you as Ephraim and as Manasseh'" (Genesis 48:20).

Jacob's prophecy, Scripture will record, comes true—the tribe of Ephraim indeed outnumbers the tribe of Manasseh (Deuteronomy 33:17 records a portion of Moses' blessing of the 12 tribes: "They are the ten thousands of Ephraim, and they are the thousands of Manasseh"). Ephraim also outstrips his older brother in greatness—when the 10 northern tribes of Israel later split from Judah and Benjamin (after King Solomon, David's son, dies), the name of the tribe of Ephraim becomes synonymous with the nation of Israel.

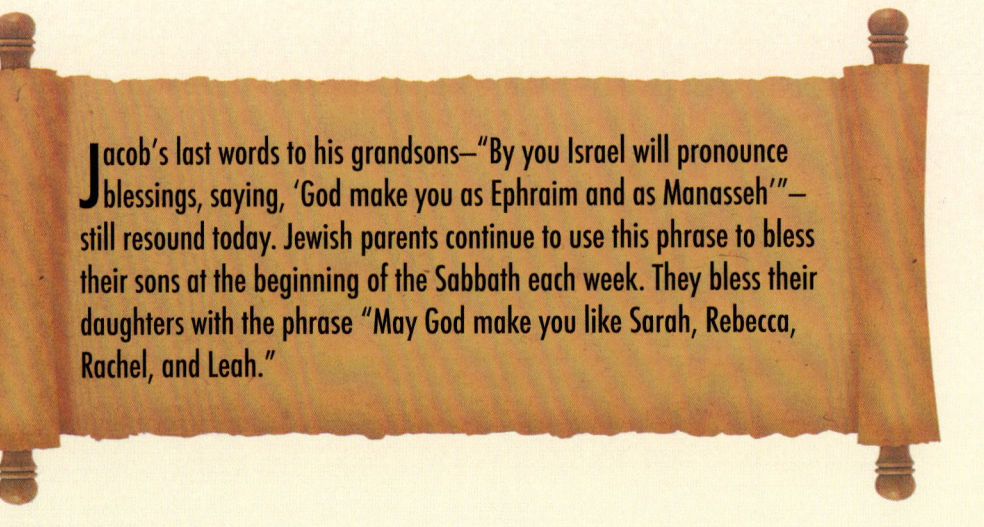

Jacob's last words to his grandsons—"By you Israel will pronounce blessings, saying, 'God make you as Ephraim and as Manasseh'"—still resound today. Jewish parents continue to use this phrase to bless their sons at the beginning of the Sabbath each week. They bless their daughters with the phrase "May God make you like Sarah, Rebecca, Rachel, and Leah."

10

LAST DAYS

After he blesses Ephraim and Manasseh and immediately before he dies, Jacob gathers his sons to himself and issues a prophecy and blessing to each one. Judah and Joseph receive the longest and most bountiful blessings. About Judah—the brother who had become a leader in the absence of the oldest son and who had spoken passionately to Joseph on behalf of Benjamin—Jacob prophesies that "the scepter shall not depart from Judah, nor the ruler's staff from between his feet" (Genesis 49:10). The tribe of Judah later becomes the largest of the 12 tribes of Israel, and the line of Christ flows through his descendants.

As for Joseph, Jacob blesses him as follows:

> Joseph is a fruitful bough,
>   a fruitful bough by a spring;
>   his branches run over the wall.
> The archers bitterly attacked him,

> shot at him, and harassed him severely,
> yet his bow remained unmoved;
> his arms were made agile
> by the hands of the Mighty One of Jacob
> (from there is the Shepherd, the Stone of Israel),
> by the God of your father who will help you,
> by the Almighty who will bless you
> with blessings of heaven above,
> blessings of the deep that crouches beneath,
> blessings of the breasts and of the womb.
> The blessings of your father
> are mighty beyond the blessings of my parents,
> up to the bounties of the everlasting hills.
> May they be on the head of Joseph,
> and on the brow of him who was set apart from his
> brothers. (Genesis 49:22–26)

The blessing is a review of Joseph's life and a reiteration of God's blessing and direction upon it, as well as a confirmation that Joseph is "set apart from his brothers."

After Jacob blesses his sons, he repeats his desire to be buried with his fathers in Canaan. He gives specific directions, saying, "I am to be gathered to my people; bury me with my fathers in the cave that is in the field of Ephron the Hittite, in the cave that is in the field at Machpelah, to the east of Mamre, in the land of Canaan, which Abraham bought with the field from Ephron the Hittite to possess as a burying place. There they buried Abraham and Sarah his wife. There they buried Isaac and Rebekah his wife, and there I buried Leah—the field and the cave that is in it were bought from the Hittites" (Genesis 49:29–32). The longing to be with his fathers, in the land that God had promised to them, stays with Jacob (Israel) until the very end. After Jacob finishes directing his sons, he "breathed his last and was gathered to his people" (Genesis 49:33). Joseph falls on his father's face, weeping over him and kissing him.

JACOB'S BURIAL

When a patriarch in ancient societies died, his people would gather together to grieve for him and pay their respects. Depending on the greatness of the individual, the mourning process could last for many days. Such is the case with the death of Jacob.

Joseph calls Egypt's physicians (medical men, not practitioners of the mystical arts) to embalm his father. The embalming, or mummifying, process in Egypt (one of the first countries to introduce the practice) took about 40 days; the body had to be gutted, dried, and wrapped. According to Jewish legend, Joseph makes use of his riches and power to honor his father by ordering his body to be laid on a "couch of ivory, covered with gold, studded with gems, and hung with drapery of byssus and purple. Fragrant wine was poured out at its side, and aromatic spices burnt next to it."

After the embalming is complete, the Israelites and Egyptians continue their mourning for another month, for a total of 70 days. Diodorus, an ancient writer, says 72 days was the customary period of mourning for a king. So great is the Egyptians' admiration for Jacob that they accord him almost the same privilege as one of their own kings.

Once the mourning is complete, Joseph asks Pharaoh to let him honor Jacob's last wish—that he be buried with his family in Canaan. It is a measure of Pharaoh's esteem for Joseph that he grants the request. But Joseph is not the only one going on the trip: "With him went up all the servants of Pharaoh, the elders of his household, and all the elders of the land of Egypt, as well as all the household of Joseph, his brothers, and his father's household. Only their children, their flocks, and their herds were left in the land of Goshen. And there went up with him both chariots and horsemen. It was a very great company" (Genesis 50:7–9). This grand funeral procession includes everyone from high-ranking Egyptian officials to Hebrew shepherds. Jewish legend again tells of the luxuriant trappings that Joseph provides: The bier on which Jacob's body rests "was fashioned of pure gold, the border thereof inlaid with onyx stones and bdellium, and the cover was gold woven work joined to the bier with threads that were held together with hooks of onyx stones and bdellium. Joseph placed a large golden crown upon the head of his father, and a golden sceptre he put in his hand, arraying him like a living king."

The procession continues to a place called Atad in Canaan, where it halts for seven more days of a "very great and grievous lamentation" (Genesis 50:10). The Canaanites see the magnitude of the Egyptians' grief over the death of Jacob and change the name of the threshing floor from Atad to Abel-Mizraim ("the mourning of Egypt" or "the meadow of Egypt"). Jacob's sons continue the journey and fulfill their promise to their father by burying him in the ancestral burying place—the cave at Machpelah, alongside Abraham and Sarah, Isaac and Rebekah, and his own wife Leah. Their task finished, Joseph, his brothers, and all who have made the journey with them return to Egypt.

ONE LAST SUSPICION

Once they settle back into their everyday lives in Egypt, Joseph's brothers begin to wonder about Joseph's true attitude toward them. Does he harbor hatred against them for the horrendous way they treated him so many years ago? What if Joseph has simply been waiting for their father to die to take his revenge?

The brothers send a message to Joseph, telling him that before he died, Jacob had commanded them to say to

Mummification

By the time of Joseph, Egyptians had made extensive use of the process of embalming, or mummification. The goal of the process was to remove all moisture from the body so that it would not easily decay. To accomplish this, special priests with extensive knowledge of human anatomy would remove all the internal organs except the heart, which Egyptians believed was the center of a person's being. These organs were preserved separately in canopic jars that were buried with the body.

To remove moisture from the body, embalmers would then cover it with natron, a type of salt with drying properties. Once the body was dried out, the priests could fill any sunken areas with linen to make it seem more lifelike. The final step involved wrapping the body with hundreds of yards of linen. The embalmers sometimes wrapped fingers and toes separately and would often place a mask of the person's face between the layers of the head wrappings. The expense prohibited many common people from undergoing the process, so mummification was reserved mainly for pharaohs, officials, and members of the nobility.

Egyptians considered the body the soul's home. They believed that at the time of death, a person's soul would leave his or her body. But the soul could rejoin the body after burial and survive in the afterlife—provided that the soul recognized the body. Thus it was crucial that the body be preserved in as lifelike a state as possible.

An Egyptian mummy on display at the Cairo Museum, Egypt.

This building stands over the ancient cave tomb where Jacob is believed to have been buried, along with his grandparents Abraham and Sarah, and his parents, Isaac and Rebekah. Jews, Christians, and Muslims consider the Cave of the Patriarchs a holy site; according to Muslim tradition, the bones of Joseph were eventually buried here as well.

Joseph, "Please forgive the transgressions of your brothers and their sin, because they did evil to you" (Genesis 50:17). They also ask full absolution for their deeds, saying, "Please forgive the transgression of the servants of the God of your father" (Genesis 50:17). Their guilty consciences have returned to eat away at their certain knowledge of Joseph's forgiveness.

Joseph weeps before his brothers and tells them not to fear, for he has not taken God's place as a judge. He then utters one of the most famous statements in Jewish history, offering a rationale for his kind treatment of them: "As for you, you meant evil against me, but God meant it for good" (Genesis 50:20). One scholar suggests that Joseph's "wise, theological answer has gone down in history as the classic statement of God's sovereignty over the affairs of men." Joseph sees clearly that even though his brothers' actions against him were evil, they were the means by which the descendants of Jacob (the nation of Israel) have been kept alive. Joseph assures his brothers that he will continue to provide for them and their families.

THE DEATH OF JOSEPH

And provide for them he does, until he is 110 years old. The Bible is relatively quiet about the last 54 years of Joseph's life. Genesis 50:23 relates that he became a great-grandfather: "And Joseph saw Ephraim's children of the third generation. The children also of Machir the son of Manasseh were counted as Joseph's own." The text in Hebrew literally means that Machir's sons were born on Joseph's knees. He has become a patriarch in his own right, one who loves his family and stays close to them.

Presumably, he continues to rule over the land of Egypt as Pharaoh's vizier. According to Jewish legend, Pharaoh dies when Joseph is 71. Some Egyptians desire to make Joseph king rather than letting Pharaoh's son assume the throne, but they are opposed by others who object to having a foreigner on the throne. Pharaoh's son is thus given the title, yet Joseph continues as vizier of Egypt; he also reigns as king over lands he has conquered outside of Egypt, with the people bringing him yearly tributes. The legend continues that Joseph rules this way for 40 years, "beloved of all, and respected by the Egyptians and the other nations, and during all that time his brethren dwelt in Goshen, happy and blithe in the service of God."

Before he dies at the age of 110—an age considered by Egyptians of the time to be an ideal lifespan—Joseph calls his brothers together and says to them, "I am about to die, but God will visit [take care of] you and bring you up out of this land to the land that he swore to Abraham, to Isaac, and to Jacob" (Genesis 50:24). Joseph does not want his brothers to worry after he is gone, and he wants their faith in the God of their fathers to remain strong. Then, reminiscent of his father, he makes the sons of Israel swear, saying, "God will surely visit [take care of] you and you shall carry up my bones from here" (Genesis 50:25). These are the last recorded words of Joseph, and in them the faith that has characterized his life is still plainly evident. Hebrews 11:22, the Jewish "Hall of Faith," says about Joseph, "By faith Joseph, at the end of his life, made mention of the exodus of the Israelites and gave directions concerning his bones." He knows God has promised to bring the nation of Israel back to Canaan, and his dying wish is that he should also be returned to his homeland. He truly believes this will happen, and in the end, it does.

Immediately after Joseph dies, he is embalmed and placed in a coffin; some 350 years later, Moses leads the Israelites on their exodus from Egypt through the Red Sea

> The ancient book of Jubilees reports that Joseph asked his people to wait to carry his body to Canaan. At the time of his death, the book says, the Egyptians were fighting a war with the king of Canaan, which had effectively sealed the borders: "and the gate of Egypt was shut, and no one went out of Egypt and no one went in. And Joseph died . . . and they buried him in the land of Egypt" (Jubilees 46:6-8).

Last Days 111

Exodus 1:8 says that after Joseph's death, a new king arose who "did not know Joseph." This new pharaoh pressed the Israelites into slavery, eventually leading to the exodus.

into the wilderness. Exodus 13:19 is the fulfillment of the promise Joseph had insisted upon before he died: "Moses took the bones of Joseph with him, for Joseph had made the sons of Israel solemnly swear, saying, 'God will surely visit you, and you shall carry up my bones with you from here.'" After wandering through the wilderness for 40 years and testing their relationship with God all the while, the Israelites reenter and conquer the Promised Land (now called Israel) under the leadership of Joshua. After Joshua dies and is buried, Joseph's bones are finally buried as well. They have been carried along the entire journey—more than 40 years—before finally being put to rest in the land God had promised to his people. According to Joshua 24:32–33, "As for the bones of Joseph, which the people of Israel brought up from

Michelangelo's sculpture of Moses, who the Bible says brought Joseph's bones out of Egypt in accordance with Joseph's dying wish.

According to Jewish tradition, Joseph's bones were buried at the Canaanite village of Shechem, where his father, Jacob, had owned a piece of land. The village was near the modern city of Nablus in Israel. The photo above shows the high place (or altar) at Shechem, where the ancient Israelites would have worshipped God.

Egypt, they buried them at Shechem, in the piece of land that Jacob bought from the sons of Hamor the father of Shechem for a hundred pieces of money. It became an inheritance of the descendants of Joseph."

A Jewish legend says that during their wanderings in the desert, the Israelites carried two shrines with them: the Ark of the Covenant, containing the stone tablets with the Ten Commandments; and the coffin containing Joseph's bones. According to the legend, "The wayfarers who saw the two receptacles wondered, and they would ask, 'How doth the ark of the dead come next to the ark of the Everliving?' The answer was, 'The dead man enshrined in the one fulfilled the commandments enshrined in the other.'"

FINAL ANALYSIS

Joseph is an important figure in the Old Testament; his life plays a crucial role in the fulfillment of God's covenant with the Jewish people. Only Joseph's rise to power in Egypt enables the young nation of Israel to avoid starvation. And after Joseph brings his family to Egypt, the Israelites flourish: the 70 original settlers have increased to 603,000 men age 20 and over (and probably around 2 million people in all) by the time the entire nation of Israel marches out of Egypt some 400 years later.

Joseph is a moral hero, a man anyone can admire, regardless of his or her faith. As one scholar says, "His withstanding of temptation, his calm endurance of wrong, his silence as to Potiphar's wife, and his faithfulness in every duty, constituted a noble victory—one of the noblest in Scripture." He is remembered as Joseph the Righteous because he faces his entire life with an attitude of unshakeable trust that the God of his fathers will not abandon him—and even more, is orchestrating every event in his life for good purposes.

Notes

CHAPTER 2: GROWING UP

page 21: "Abraham and the other patriarchs . . ." David Noel Freeman, editor, *The Anchor Bible Dictionary* (New York: Doubleday, 1992), p. 1077.

page 23: "beauty of his body . . ." Flavius Josephus, *The Complete Works of Flavius Josephus* (Philadelphia: John E. Potter and Company, 1887?), p. 51.

page 23: "resembled his father . . ." Louis Ginzberg, *Legends of the Bible* (Philadelphia and Jerusalem: The Jewish Publication Society, 1956), p. 194.

page 23: "It was not unnatural . . ." William G. Blaikie, *Heroes of Israel: Abraham, Isaac, Jacob, Joseph & Moses* (Birmingham, AL: Solid Ground Christian Books, 2005), pp. 237–238.

page 24: "affection of his [Joseph's] father . . ." Josephus, *Complete Works*, p. 51.

page 25: "spoiled brat . . ." Rabbi Joseph Telushkin, *Jewish Literacy: The Most Important Things to Know About the Jewish Religion, Its People, and Its History* (New York: William Morrow, 1991), p. 41.

CHAPTER 3: BETRAYAL AND SLAVERY

page 30: "In such a place . . ." Dods, quoted in Blaikie, *Heroes of Israel*, pp. 239–240.

page 32: "[Judah,] seeing some Arabians . . ." Josephus, *Complete Works*, p. 82.

page 34: "and they sold Joseph . . ." Targum Pseudo-Jonathan, Genesis 37:28, quoted *inter alia* in James L. Kugel, *The Bible as It Was* (Cambridge, Mass., and London: The Belknap Press of Harvard University Press), p. 251.

page 34: "Nothing has ever happened . . ." Philo of Alexandria, *The Works of Philo*, trans. by C. D. Yonge (Peabody, Mass.: Hendrickson Publishers, 1993), p. 437.

page 35–36: "body emitted a pleasant smell . . ." Ginzberg, *Legends of the Bible*, pp. 203–204.

page 37: "That there was something superior . . ." Blaikie, *Heroes of Israel*, p. 241.

CHAPTER 4: THE HOUSE OF POTIPHAR

page 41: "they all cut their hands . . ." Ginzberg, *Legends of the Bible*, pp. 217–218.

page 42: "Though thou coverest . . ." Ibid., p. 216.

CHAPTER 5: THE PRISONER WHO INTERPRETS DREAMS

page 50: "Seeing the youth's zeal . . ." Ginzberg, *Legends of the Bible*, p. 223.

page 54: "It became clear . . ." Blaikie, *Heroes of Israel*, p. 248.

page 57: "I desire thee to suppress . . ." Josephus, *Complete Works*, p. 55.

CHAPTER 6: FROM SLAVE TO RULER

page 62: "Musicians, no less than . . ." Ginzberg, *Legends of the Bible*, p. 231.

page 62–63: "In the rabbinic *midrash* . . ." Rabbi Joseph Telushkin, *Biblical Literacy: The Most Important People, Events, and Ideas of the Hebrew Bible* (New York: William Morrow, 1997), p. 81.

page 63: "Never had there been . . ." Blaikie, *Heroes of Israel*, p. 250.

page 68: "The poor ate carrion . . ." Stanley, quoted in Blaikie, *Heroes of Israel*, p. 256.

page 69: "Nor did he open . . ." Josephus, *Complete Works*, p. 56.

Chapter 7: The Brothers Return

page 72: "It was not God's will . . ." Philo, *On Joseph* 165, quoted in Kugel, *The Bible as It Was*, p. 266.

page 73: "And at this crisis . . ." Philo of Alexandria, *On Joseph*, from *The Works of Philo Judaeus*, translated by Charles D. Yonge. Available at http://www.earlychristianwritings.com/yonge/book23.html

page 79: "entertained his mother's son . . ." Philo, *On Joseph* 232–235, quoted in Kugel, *The Bible as It Was*, p. 267.

Chapter 8: Joseph Revealed

page 84: "In the thousands of years . . ." Telushkin, *Biblical Literacy*, p. 87.

page 86: "I am Joseph . . ." Telushkin, *Jewish Literacy*, p. 42.

page 87: "Do not, therefore . . ." Josephus, *Complete Works*, p. 60.

Chapter 9: Israelites in Egypt

page 95: "Its fields are full . . ." Panbesa in *Records of Past* vi. 11, quoted in Blaikie, *Heroes of Israel*, p. 273.

page 102: "May God make you . . ." Telushkin, *Biblical Literacy*, p. 90.

Chapter 10: Last Days

page 105: "couch of ivory . . ." Ginzberg, *Legends of the Bible*, p. 259.

page 106: "was fashioned . . ." Ibid., p. 261.

page 109: "wise, theological answer . . ." John MacArthur, *The MacArthur Study Bible* (Nashville, Tenn.: Nelson Bibles, a division of Thomas Nelson Publishers, 2006), p. 88.

page 109: "beloved of all . . ." Ginzberg, *Legends of the Bible*, p. 264.

page 112–13: "The wayfarers who saw . . ." Ibid., p. 265.

page 113: "His withstanding of temptation . . ." Blaikie, *Heroes of Israel*, p. 252.

Glossary

apocryphal—relating to the Apocrypha, a collection of early Jewish writings excluded from the canon of the Hebrew Scriptures; Jewish and Christian works resembling biblical books, but not included among the Apocrypha, are collected in the Pseudepigrapha (including Joseph and Asenath, the book of Jubilees, and the Testaments of Jacob's sons).

Canaan—an ancient region made up of Palestine or the part of it between the Jordan River and the Mediterranean Sea.

Haggadah—traditional Jewish literature, especially the nonlegal part of the Talmud.

Midrash—any of a group of Jewish commentaries on the Hebrew Scriptures compiled between 400 and 1200 C.E.

patrilineal—relating to, based on, or tracing ancestral descent through the paternal line.

pharaoh—a king of ancient Egypt.

Qur'an—the sacred text of Islam, considered by Muslims to contain the revelations of God to the prophet Muhammad.

Semitic—characteristic of any of a number of peoples of ancient southwestern Asia, including the Hebrews, Arabs, Phoenicians, and Akkadians; of, relating to, or constituting a subgroup of the Afro-Asiatic language group that includes Arabic, Hebrew, Amharic, and Aramaic.

shekel—any of several ancient units of weight, especially a Hebrew unit equal to about a half ounce; a gold or silver coin equal in weight to one of these units, especially the chief silver coin of the ancient Hebrews.

Sheol—the abode of the dead in ancient Hebrew thought.

soothsayer—one who claims to be able to foretell events or predict the future; a seer.

Targum—a general name for a translation of the Hebrew Bible into Aramaic, a Semitic language related to Hebrew and spoken widely throughout the ancient Near East.

Torah—the first five books of the Hebrew Scriptures (Genesis, Exodus, Leviticus, Numbers, and Deuteronomy).

vizier—a civil officer in ancient Egypt who had powers akin to those of a viceroy.

Further Reading

BOOKS FOR YOUNG READERS

Davidson, Josephine. *The Old Testament: Ten Plays for Readers Theater* (Bellingham, WA: The Right Book Company, 1992).

Harris, Geraldine. *Cultural Atlas for Young People: Ancient Egypt* (New York: Facts On File, Inc., 2003).

Wildsmith, Brian. *Joseph* (Grand Rapids, MI: Eerdmans Books for Young Readers, 1997).

BOOKS FOR ADULTS

Blaikie, William G. *Heroes of Israel: Abraham, Isaac, Jacob, Joseph & Moses* (Birmingham, AL: Solid Ground Christian Books, 2005).

Fatoohi, Louay. *The Prophet Joseph in the Qur'an, the Bible, and History* (Birmingham, UK: Luna Plena Publishing, 2007).

Ginzberg, Louis. *Legends of the Bible* (Philadelphia and Jerusalem: The Jewish Publication Society, 1956).

Josephus, Flavius. *The Complete Works of Flavius Josephus* (Philadelphia: John E. Potter and Company, 1887?).

Kaltner, John. *Inquiring of Joseph: Getting to Know a Biblical Character Through the Qur'an* (Collegeville, MN: The Liturgical Press, 2003).

MacArthur, John. *The MacArthur Study Bible* (Nashville, Tenn.: Nelson Bibles, a division of Thomas Nelson Publishers, 2006).

Swindoll, Charles R. *Joseph: A Man of Integrity and Forgiveness* (Nashville, TN: Thomas Nelson Publishers, 1998).

Telushkin, Rabbi Joseph. *Biblical Literacy: The Most Important People, Events, and Ideas of the Hebrew Bible* (New York: William Morrow, 1997).

———. *Jewish Literacy: The Most Important People, Events, and Ideas of the Hebrew Bible* (New York: William Morrow, 1997).

Internet Resources

http://www.ancientegypt.co.uk/
The British Museum's Web site dedicated to ancient Egypt.

http://www.jewishencyclopedia.com
The complete contents of the 12-volume *Jewish Encyclopedia*, originally published 1901–1906, includes much information on Joseph.

http://www.myjewishlearning.com
This Web site provides well-written historical and scholarly information about Judaism, including articles about Joseph.

http://www.nationalgeographic.com/pyramids
National Geographic magazine's site dedicated to ancient Egypt includes photos, diagrams, news stories, interactive features, and links.

http://www.sacred-texts.com
The Internet Sacred Text Archive has an enormous repository of electronic texts about religion, mythology, legends and folklore, and occult and esoteric topics. Texts related to Joseph include the works of Josephus; *The Legends of the Jews*, by Louis Ginzberg; and the Pseudepigrapha, including the Testaments of Jacob's 12 sons.

Index

Abel-Mizraim, 106
Abraham, 7–8, 17, 22, 31, 86, 90, 94, 98, 104, 106, *108*
   and the covenant with God, 13–14, 18, 91, 99, 112–113
Abram. *See* Abraham
Absalom, 41
Alma-Tadema, Lawrence (Sir), *61*
Amos, 9, 34
animals. *See* livestock
Anpu (Anepu, Anubis), 47
Ark of the Covenant, 112
   See also covenant, Abraham's (with God)
Asenath (Joseph's wife), 63–65
Asher (Joseph's brother), 20, 71
Atad, 106

barter, 21
Bata, 47
Beersheba, 90–91
Benjamin, 19–20, 21, 23, 31, 72, 75, 77–79, 88, 102
   Jacob's favoritism of, 24, 71
   and Joseph's silver cup, 81–83
Bilhah, 19, 22, 25
book of Jubilees, 44, 110

Cairo Museum, *107*
Canaan, 17, 20, 22, 36, 77, 87–88, 99
   burial of Jacob in, 104–106
   famine in, 6, 69, 70–71, 92, 96
   map, 76
   as the Promised Land, 13, 90–91, 94, 100, 110
Cave of the Patriarchs, *108*
Christianity, 11, *14*, 84, *108*
Chronicles, 99–100
   See also Old Testament books
coat of many colors, 12, 22–24, 25, 29, 33, *34*
   See also Joseph
covenant, Abraham's (with God), 13–14, 18, 91, 99, 112–113
   See also Abraham
currency, 35
   See also wealth

Dan (Joseph's brother), 20, 71
Daniel, 53
David (King), 41, 102
Deuteronomy, 102
   See also Old Testament books
Dinah (Joseph's sister), 20, 22, 28
Diodorus, 105
Doré, Gustave, *19*
Dothan, 28, 30
dream interpretation, 12, 14, 25–26, 50–53, 54–59
   See also Joseph

Egypt, 17, 30, 35, 86, 87–89, 106–107, 113

Numbers in ***bold italics*** refer to captions.

artwork from, *10*
beauty techniques, 43
estates in, 39–40
famine in, 6, 12, 13–14, 16, 57–58, 66–69, 70, 85–86, 95–99
granaries, 66–67
historical time periods in, 36
Jacob travels to, 90–95
Joseph's arrival in, 36–37
map, 76
and mummification, 105, 107
record-keeping in, 68
slaves in, 31
"Story of Two Brothers" legend, 47
See also Joseph; Pharaoh
embalming, 105, 107
Ephraim (Joseph's son), 65, 98, 99–103, 109
Esau (Jacob's brother), 6, 13, 17, 20–21, 33, 77, 100
Exodus (book of), 91, 111
See also Old Testament books

faith
 Joseph's trust in God, 15, 39, 53–54, 58, 65
 and wealth, 7–9
famine, 6, 16, 70–73, 77, 85–86, 92, 95–99
 Joseph's prediction of, 12, 13–14, 57–58
 preparations for, 66–69
folktales, Jewish. *See* legends, Jewish
forgiveness, 12–13, 15, 86, 109

Gad (Joseph's brother), 20, 25, 33, 71
Genesis passages, 15–16, 95
 Abraham, 7, 18, 22
 covenant with God, 13, 18
 famine, *67*, 68–69, 96, 98
 Jacob, 20, 21, 33, 106
 Jacob in Canaan, 70
 Jacob's blessing on Manasseh and Ephraim, 99, 100–101, 102
 Jacob's blessings, 103–104
 Jacob's journey to Egypt, 90
 Joseph and his brothers, 22–23, 27, 29, 34, 71, 108–109, 110
 Joseph and Zuleika (Potiphar's wife), 41, 42, 44, *45*
 Joseph as viceroy, 59, 60
 Joseph reveals himself to his brothers, 84–85
 Joseph sends for Jacob, 87, 89
 Joseph tests his brothers, 81–83
 Joseph's arrival in Egypt, 36–37
 Joseph's children, 65
 Joseph's dream interpretations, 56, 57, 58, 66
 Joseph's faith, 15
 Joseph's imprisonment, 49–50, 51, 52, 53, 54
 Joseph's physical appearance, 40–41
 Joseph's time in Egypt, 38–39
 Joseph's wealth, 6
 reunion of Joseph and his brothers, 71–72, 74–75, 77, 78–79
 reunion of Joseph with Jacob, 92, 94
 wealth, 7–8
 See also Old Testament books
goats. *See* livestock
Goshen, 37, 87, 91–92, 95, 98–99, 109
 See also Egypt
granaries, 66–67

Hagar, 31
Haggadah, 16
 See also legends, Jewish
Hebrews, 110
 See also Old Testament books
Heliopolis (On), 37, 63–64
Hyksos, 36

Isaac (Jacob's father), 13, 17, 33, 90, 94, 100, 106, *108*
Isaiah, 9
Ishmael (Abraham's son), 31
Islam, 11, *14*, *108*
Israel (nation), 8–9, 11, 13–14, *20*, 84, 90–91, 111, 113
 naming of, 21
 twelve tribes of, 13, 100, 102, 103

Issachar (Joseph's brother), 20, 71

Jacob (Joseph's father), 11, 13, 27, 84, 86
   believes Joseph dead, 33, *34*
   blessing of, on Joseph, 103–104
   blessing of, on Manasseh and Ephraim, 98–102
   blindness of, 88, 100
   burial of, 105–106
   children of, 12, 13, 19–20, 22–23
   death of, 104–105
   early life of, 17–19
   during the famine, 70–71, 75, 77–78
   favoritism of, toward Joseph, 12, 19–20, 22–26
   is sent for by Joseph, 87–89
   parenting style, 22–23
   reunion of, with Joseph, 91–95
   travels to Egypt, 90–92
   wealth of, 6, 20–22
   wrestles an angel, 21
   See also Joseph
Jesus Christ, 7, 84
jewelry, Egyptian, *43*
Jewish Antiquities (Josephus), 32
John XXIII (Pope), 86
Joseph, 11, 13–14
   birth of, 19
   burial of, 110–113
   buries Jacob in Canaan, 105–106
   children of, 65, 78, 81, 98, 99–103, 109
   and the coat of many colors, 12, 22–24, 25, 29, 33, *34*
   death of, 109–110
   and dream interpretation, 12, 14, 26–27, 50–53, 54–58
   and forgiveness, 12–13, 15, 86–87, 109
   and God's favor, 49–50
   honesty of, 6
   is imprisoned, 44–45, 47–48, 49–55
   is sold into slavery, 31–37
   Jacob's blessing of, 103–104
   as Jacob's favorite, 12, 19–20, 22–26
   marries Asenath, 63–65
   perfumed odor of, 35–36
   personality of, 25
   physical appearance of, 40–41
   as Potiphar's slave, 38–45
   relationship of, with his brothers, 23–26, 27, 28–34, 69, 106, 108–109
   reunion of, with his brothers, 70–75, 78–79, 84–86
   reunion of, with Jacob, 91–95
   sends for Jacob, 87–89
   tests his brothers, 80–85
   thrown into a well, 29–30
   trust of, in God, 15, 39, 53–54, 58, 65
   as viceroy of Egypt, 6, 12, 16, 59–63, 65–69, 95–99, 109
   wealth of, 6, 62–63
   as "Zaphenath-paneah," 63
   and Zuleika (Potiphar's wife), 41–48
   See also Egypt; Jacob (Joseph's father)
"Joseph's barns" (pyramids), 66
Josephus, 23–24, 29, *32*, 57, 63, 69, 72, 86–87
Joshua, 111–112
Jubilees (book of), 44, 110
Judah (Joseph's brother), 20, 71, 91, 102, 108
   proposes selling Joseph, 31, 32
   protects Benjamin, 77, 82–84, 103
Judaism, 11, 13, *14*, 15, 65, 84

Keturah, 31
Koran. *See* Qur'an

Laban, 18, *19*, 20
Leah (Jacob's wife), 18–19, 23, 102, 104, 106
legends, Jewish, 6, 8, 15–16, 37, 41, 42, 50, 53, 70, 78, 112
   Egyptian famine, 67
   Jacob's burial, 106
   Joseph and Asenath, 64

Joseph as viceroy, 62–63
Joseph tests his brothers, 80–81
Levi (Joseph's brother), 20, 22, 71, 100
livestock, 6, 20–21, 25, 91–92, **94**, 96
Lot, 98

Machir (Joseph's grandson), 109
Maimonides, Moses, 84
makeup, 43
Manasseh (Joseph's son), 65, 78, 81, 98, 99–103, 109
map
    Egypt and Canaan, 76
Mesopotamia, 18, 21
Michelangelo, *111*
Midian, 31
Midrash, 16, 62
    See also legends, Jewish
money. *See* wealth
Moses, 95, 102, 110–111
mummification, 105, 107

Nablus, *112*
Naphtali (Joseph's brother), 20, 71
Nile River, 54, 67–68

Old Testament books, 7–8, 11, 15–16, 53, 91, 98, 99–100, 102
    See also Genesis passages
On (Heliopolis), 37, 63–64

Paddanaram, 18
papyrus, 68
Pentephres (Potiphera), 63–64
Pharaoh, 36, 96–99, 109
    appoints Joseph as viceroy, 59–63
    cupbearer and baker of, 50–53
    dreams of, 54–59
    and the famine, 68–69
    and Joseph's family, 87–88, 92, 94, 105
    Joseph's work for, 12, 14, 16
    See also Egypt
Philo of Alexandria, 6, **34**, 72, **73**, 79
Potiphar, 36–37, 38–48, 50, 63
Potiphera (Pentephres), 63–64
precious metals, 35
    See also wealth
pyramids, 66

Qur'an, 15–16, 39, 51, 53, 70, 86
    Jacob's blindness, 88
    Jacob's favoritism of Joseph, 24–25
    Joseph's physical appearance, 41
    Potiphar's opinion of Joseph, 37
    Potiphar's wife, 45, 47

Rachel (Jacob's wife), 18–20, 21, 23, 75, 102
Rameses, 95
Re (sun god), 64
Rebekah (Isaac's wife), 102, 104, 106, *108*
Reuben (Joseph's brother), 20, 23, 31, 33, 71, 74–75, 79
    prevents murder of Joseph, 29
    sleeps with Bilhah, 22, 99–100

Sarah (Abraham's wife), 102, 104, 106, *108*
Septuagint, 98
    See also Old Testament books
Sermon on the Mount, 7
Shechem, 22, 28–29, 112
sheep. *See* livestock
shekels, 35
    See also wealth
Simeon (Joseph's brother), 20, 22, 33, 71, 74–75, 79, 99
    testament of, 24, 87
slavery, 30–37
Solomon (King), 8, 102
sphinx, **39**
Stephen, 98
"Story of Two Brothers," 47
Syria, 30

Talmud, 16
    See also legends, Jewish
Tanakh (Jewish Bible), 16
    See also Old Testament books
Tanis, 37, 95
taxes, 97
Telushkin, Rabbi Joseph, 84
Ten Commandments, 112

Testament of Gad, 25
Testament of Joseph, 42–43
Testament of Simeon, 24, 87
Thévenin, Charles, *85*
Torah, 16, 42, 82–83, 84
   See also Old Testament books
trade routes, 30–31

Valley of Hebron, 28

wealth
   and faith, 7–9
   given to Joseph by Pharaoh, 62–63
   livestock, 6, 20–21
   and precious metals, 35
The World Chronicle, **93**

Yosef ha-Tzaddik ("Joseph the Righteous"). *See* Joseph

Zaphenath-paneah. *See* Joseph
Zebulun (Joseph's brother), 20, 33–34, 71
Zilpah, 19, 22, 25
Zoan, 37, 95
Zuleika (Potiphar's wife), 41–48

Illustration Credits

2: Erich Lessing/Art Resource, NY
10: Erich Lessing/Art Resource, NY
14: Scala/Art Resource, NY
19: © 2008 JupiterImages Corp.
20: used under license from Shutterstock, Inc.
26: used under license from Shutterstock, Inc.
29: Erich Lessing/Art Resource, NY
32: Réunion des Musées Nationaux/Art Resource, NY
34: Scala/Art Resource, NY
39: used under license from Shutterstock, Inc.
40: Erich Lessing/Art Resource, NY
43: © 2008 JupiterImages Corp.
45: Erich Lessing/Art Resource, NY
46: Erich Lessing/Art Resource, NY
52: © 2008 JupiterImages Corp.
55: Erich Lessing/Art Resource, NY
56: Erich Lessing/Art Resource, NY
61: Joseph, Overseer of Pharaoh's Granaries, 1874 (oil on panel) by Sir Lawrence Alma-Tadema (1836-1912) © Dahesh Museum of Art, New York, USA/The Bridgeman Art Library
64: © 2008 JupiterImages Corp.
66: © 2008 JupiterImages Corp.
67: Cameraphoto/Art Resource, NY
68: © 2008 JupiterImages Corp.
73: Time Life Pictures/Getty Images
76: OTTN Publishing
81: used under license from Shutterstock, Inc.
85: Joseph Recognised by his Brothers, 1789 (oil on canvas) by Charles Thevenin (1764-1838) ©Musee des Beaux-Arts, Angers, France/Giraudon/The Bridgeman Art Library
93: Bildarchiv Preussischer Kulturbesitz/Art Resource, NY
94: Erich Lessing/Art Resource, NY
97: used under license from Shutterstock, Inc.
101: Alinari/Art Resource, NY
107: © 2008 JupiterImages Corp.
108: used under license from Shutterstock, Inc.
111: used under license from Shutterstock, Inc.
112: Erich Lessing/Art Resource, NY

Cover photo: Joseph, Overseer of Pharaoh's Granaries, 1874 (oil on panel) by Sir Lawrence Alma-Tadema (1836-1912) © Dahesh Museum of Art, New York, USA/The Bridgeman Art Library

BENJAMIN T. HOAK is a freelance writer living in Owensboro, Kentucky, with his wife Kelsey and their sons Carter and Taylor. He has been a newspaper writer and a middle school teacher. He is a graduate of Kentucky Wesleyan College and is a fellow of the World Journalism Institute. His work has appeared in WJI's monograph series, *City Magazine,* and the *Public Life Advocate.* He is also the co-author of the forthcoming book, *A Man as Priest in His Home.*